A Guide to
Riding, Showing and Enjoying
Other People's Horses

A Guide to
Riding, Showing and Enjoying
Other People's Horses

BARBARA BURN

Drawings by Werner Rentsch

DAVID & CHARLES
Newton Abbot   London

British Library Cataloguing in Publication Data

Burn, Barbara
  A guide to riding, showing and enjoying other
  people's horses.
  1. Horsemanship
  I. Title
  798'.2   SF309

  ISBN 0–7153–8009–5

  Library of Congress Catalog Card Number
              78-19394

First published in the United States of
America as *The Horseless Rider* by St
Martin's Press, Inc, New York

Photoset by Northern Phototypesetting
              Co, Bolton
        Printed in Great Britain
by Redwood Burn Ltd, Trowbridge and
                Esher

   for David & Charles (Publishers) Ltd
   Brunel House Newton Abbot Devon

Dedicated with love to my parents, without whom this book would never have been possible.

Young men have often been ruined through owning horses . . . but never through riding them – unless, of course, they break their necks, which – taken at a gallop – is a very good death to die.

– Winston Churchill

Contents

Preface

When I was about ten years old and quite seriously infected with horse fever, I mounted a strenuous campaign to convince my parents to buy me a horse. One of my friends had succeeded in getting herself an old pony by the name of Martini and I thought that ordering a Martini of my own would be equally simple. For years I had entertained fantasies of waking up on my birthday to find a pony tied to a tree in the back garden (we didn't have a stable), but at ten I was mature enough to realize that adding a horse to the family was going to take more effort on my part than wishful thinking.

Since direct requests hadn't worked, I decided to start the campaign by using the art of suggestion. I learned to imitate my mother's handwriting, not for the purpose of forging cheques made out to the local horse dealer but in order to work the word 'horse' unobtrusively into her shopping list. (I don't know how I expected her to find a horse in the aisles of the supermarket let alone fit it into her shopping trolley, but I was pretty desperate.) Then I set about quietly making our house suitable for a horse. When my friend's pony got a new head collar, I asked for the old one, which I carefully mended and put away in my underwear drawer. When I mowed the lawn for extra cash, I'd collect all the mown grass in a heap beside the garage to use in bedding down the eventual equine. I scrounged old pails and scrubbing brushes and even designed a convincing floor plan showing how our garage could be adapted as a stable once the family car had been evicted.

Next, I proceeded to educate myself in horsekeeping. My father, in one of his routine responses to my constant request, pointed out that I wasn't strong enough even to cut the wire on

11

a bale of hay let alone handle a horse. So I spent hours practising with wire cutters and soon developed the appropriate muscles, although I was still incapable of carrying a full bucket of water without spilling it. My horse-loving aunt explained that no one who hadn't fallen off a horse at least seven times could claim to be a true horseman, so I enlisted Martini's aid and spent some fruitful sessions in the apple orchard until I became a true horseman. (Although the experience didn't do much for my riding skills, I did lose my fear of falling and I learned what it was like to have the wind knocked out of my chest – awful.)

And then I worked out the hardest part – the finances. I spent less of my allowance on sweets and records, and set aside a few pence a week in a shoebox. I worked out the cost of carrots, hay and horseshoes, and balanced the total against various family expenditures. Armed with this information, I presented my case to my parents: if they would give up drinking, they could afford to keep a horse for me. And of course, I offered to do all the work and help out as much as I could with my dollar a month.

Needless to say, it didn't work. Not only that, my mother threw out the head collar when she found it in the washing machine along with my underwear and she turned the grass heap into a compost pile. (I never found out what happened to the floor plan but it may have been what gave my father the idea to turn the one-car garage into one for two cars a year or so later.) As I grew older, my approach became somewhat more sophisticated, but they never budged. 'The neighbourhood wasn't designed to keep horses in,' they would say. 'We don't have room for a stable and paddock,' 'Who's going to feed and exercise the horse when you're away visiting friends?'

Even though I had ready answers to these arguments, I could never get around the fact that they simply weren't enthusiastic about the idea. My mother had grown up in a horsy family as the one daughter in four who was afraid of horses, and the only time my father ever rode he was arrested for trespassing. They did allow me to take an occasional riding lesson and to hang around Martini's box a lot (I think they liked his name), but for some reason they felt that straightening my teeth, buying me books and putting clothes on my back were more important contributions to my upbringing than having a horse around.

Without a horse in the garden, I had to work pretty hard at getting myself into the saddle as often as my horse fever demanded. Occasional riding lessons at the local riding stables were not nearly enough to satisfy my needs, and yet daily lessons were far too much for my budget. I learned to muck out stalls and clean tack so that I could trade my work for rides on friends' horses. I offered my services as exercise rider to horse owners with broken legs (from skiing, I told my parents) and to people who were dumb enough to find a holiday abroad more attractive than staying home with their animals. I managed to get myself sent to camps that offered riding and I ingratiated myself with counsellors who could take time off while I worked in the stables. In college I found that riding counted as a physical education credit, and I eventually got a job as an editor so that I could work on books about horses. I found stables that gave lessons in the evening and at weekends, and I got friends with cars interested in riding so that we could get out of the city. In short, I learned to hack around.

Like malaria, the horse fever never truly subsided, and 'horse' still appeared automatically at the top of my birthday and Christmas present lists, but it wasn't until I married a veterinary surgeon that the idea of getting a horse became more than just a fancy. At that point I was riding twice a week and getting interested in horse shows. When my husband looked over my birthday list, he asked 'Why *don't* we get a horse?' and I was stunned. It was possible. We could keep it at livery just outside the city, he could keep it sound and my life could be complete at last.

But then it hit me. I realized suddenly that after all these years it might just be possible that I didn't really *want* a horse. Keeping a horse at livery was expensive, my schedule was full with a house to renovate, a full-time job, four cats, two dogs and two stepchildren, and besides that I was having a pretty good time doing what I was doing. Because I had ridden many different horses, I had managed to develop a flexible riding technique and I enjoyed horses for different reasons – hacking, jumping, dressage and so on. I knew that if I tried to put all my eggs into a single equestrian basket, I'd be asking more of one animal than it could possibly deliver.

Through my work as a writer and editor I have had the chance to meet many well-known riders and trainers and to read many books written by expert horsemen. In the course of asking questions and looking for answers, I have always been surprised to find how many people have advanced far in the profession without actually having horses of their own. In fact, many of them told me that using different horses could be good for one's riding and that a single horse could be limiting. I have also been dismayed to find that most horse books were written for horse owners and not for people like me – those of us who love to ride but, for one reason or another, must ride horses belonging to others. And so I thought I might set down some advice for 'horseless' riders like myself, along with the comments, stories and suggestions from professionals in the field. It isn't always possible to make a negative situation into a positive one, but I have come to believe that *not* owning a horse can be a rewarding experience. Like any activity, riding can be expensive, but riding other people's horses is a lot cheaper than paying for upkeep, tack, veterinarians, farriers and equipment before you even get into the saddle. Horses, like all animals, require a responsible commitment of time, energy, affection and care, but if one has a full schedule, one hour of commitment a day is a lot more sensible than twenty-four. It will take effort and ingenuity to appreciate the advantages of not having a horse in the garden at your constant beck and call, but it doesn't take much imagination to see that if sickness or bad weather makes riding impossible, a horse that isn't there won't need to be exercised or fed or turned out or cleaned up after.

I can't in truth say that I will never want a horse of my own – indeed, I'm still trying to get my boss to move his company out to the country so that I can ride more frequently – but for the time being I am happy enough being a horseless rider to pass along my enthusiasm to others in the same situation. It's not a perfect life. Horses for hire are not fine specimens capable of competing in the Olympics; sometimes they aren't even capable of delivering a comfortable ride. But they can teach you a lot and, if you have a mind to do so, you can teach them something too, making a comfortable ride more likely the next time around. Hiring or borrowing a horse doesn't require you to borrow all the problems of the owner, but you do have certain responsibilities and must be willing to take certain risks when you take the horse. Knowing what these responsibilities and risks are and how to deal with them is part of the education of *any* rider, however, and learning to become expert in handling other people's horses can be an important step toward the goal of everyone who takes horses seriously – that of being a true horseman. In spite of Martini's lessons in the apple orchard, I still haven't achieved that high level, but I have discovered that proof of ownership is not necessarily a proof of horsemanship.

The first five chapters in this book are dedicated to all riders who must look beyond the back garden for a mount, and though some of the advice will be aimed at the novice, riders at all levels of expertise and experience should be able to use the information about equestrian opportunities, methods of analysing stables, instructors and horses, and ways of adapting their riding style to whatever animal comes along. Careful readers of the contents page will note that I have put the cart before the horse by discussing riding styles and instructors before exploring the local stables and their noble inhabitant the hack horse. This is a deliberate ploy on my part to convince the beginner (and even more advanced riders) that there is more to riding than just renting a horse. I have seen too many people take their first ride at public stables with no prior instruction and be so unsettled (if not actually unseated) by the experience that they determined never to ride again. This is an unfortunate situation if only because it can be so easily avoided. Since this book is not addressed to stable operators, I can only appeal to you, the horseless rider, to take that all-important step of educating yourself before you pick up the telephone directory. I don't mean that you should study the serious manuals or apply to Olympic coaches for instruction before you meet your first horse, but I do implore you to familiarize yourself with the styles of riding and the way of learning them before you get into the saddle. You wouldn't dream of driving a car on a motorway or try to ski down the Matterhorn without a lesson or two, and the same goes for horseback riding. You can hire cars, skis and horses, but you'll be doing yourself (and your fellows) a disservice if you don't know how to operate them!

The last part of the book is designed for riders who consider themselves more obsessed than occasional, those who are willing to spend more than an hour or two a week in the company of *Equus caballus*. For you I'll include ways of earning money around horses, improving your riding chances and participating in sports usually considered the exclusive domain of the horse owner. And for the hopelessly incurable, I'll describe the various professions in the field and, last but not least, that ultimate alternative to horselessness – getting a horse of your own.

1
The Rider

All horseless riders have at least two things in common – an interest in riding and a lack of the animal on which to ride – but there are a lot of differences too, in ability, ambition, available time and money, to name only a few. Before you start bemoaning the fact that there isn't a horse in your garden, try to figure out what your own problems are, work out some solutions and then start thinking like a horseless rider. I'll be willing to wager that for every problem there is not only a solution, but also a distinct advantage over the horse owner.

Horselessness Explained

First question: Why don't you have a horse? Is it a lack of money, time or expertise? Is it an unsympathetic family? A gardenless house or flat? Or is it just that your interest in riding is relatively recent and you aren't yet sure just how committed you want to become?

The best way to deal with those negative reasons is to take a positive attitude. Since it does take a minimum of money and time even to ride other people's horses, work out how much room there is in your budget and schedule and set aside the surplus for riding. One of my solutions was to sign up for a course of ten Wednesday night lessons, for which I had to pay in advance, thus getting a sizeable discount. That way my riding budget was safe from spending sprees on clothes I didn't need and my Wednesday evenings became sacred. (A couple of my non-riding friends were hurt when I turned down dinner invitations because I 'had to go riding', but they soon learned to try me on Thursdays instead.) If you find – as I did – that a weekly lesson isn't enough, there are several ways in which you can earn extra money and time to ride, which I will elaborate on in chapter 7.

Lack of expertise may be a good reason not to own a horse, but if you plan to ride, it's a good idea to overcome that lack by learning as much as possible about horses – not just how to ride them but how they are put together, cared for and trained. Even if you are at the stage where you feel you know nothing at all, there are plenty of good ways to find out. The best way to start is to ride under expert instruction, which will mean lessons at first, but you can continue or supplement that education on your own – by practising on hourly hacks, or by reading books and applying what you read to what you do, or by hanging around horses and horse people a lot. This is one area in which the horseless rider has the edge on the horse owner, who must ride the same animal all the time. Kathy Kusner, a former member of the U.S. Equestrian Team, worked as a dealer's rider early in her career, showing off hundreds of animals to prospective buyers. 'This was marvellous experience,' she reports, 'and so many horses did a lot to make riding become almost as natural as breathing. . . . Maybe it wasn't very classical or conservative, but it was a very practical education.'

The well-known equestrian writer R. S. Summerhays points out in his *Elements of Riding* that: 'The best horsemen are those who have ridden many horses, and if you have the ambition to succeed as a horseman, you must ride a number of horses; in fact, all the horses that come your way. Seek them out and ride them, all the different ones you can, of all shapes and of all sizes.'

Bill Steinkraus, Olympic gold-medal winner and a leading American rider for years, points out that 'spoiled horses, difficult horses, and even rogues, can teach us much that is important; the rider who is too well mounted may never really learn to ride'.

If your main problem is that your family thinks you are crazy for wanting to ride, take heart. Even if they won't let you add a horse to the household, you should be able to convince them that you are serious enough to deserve some support – whether that means giving you money or time off or simply keeping their mouths shut when you put on your riding clothes. Bill Steinkraus recalls:

> Neither of my parents was a rider, and it always seemed to me as a child that my strange passion for horses was more tolerated than encouraged – in any case, I never seemed able to do as much riding as I would have liked. . . . But I am grateful to them for not having permitted me to become too early saturated with riding, or to regard riding as more of an obligation than a treat. So many children of fine horsemen, who get every encouragement from their parents to follow in their footsteps lose their enthusiasm for riding very early because the riding is so *available*, and too easily a matter of 'If you don't exercise your pony today, you can't watch television before dinner'.

So even if it infuriates you that your parents or your spouse or your children giggle uncontrollably every time you pull on your boots (or, worse, resent the fact that you have your own 'thing'), don't despair. They'll be delighted when you come home with your first blue rosette.

Perhaps you have time, money, expertise and an encouraging family, but you don't have any place to keep a horse. Suburban areas are often not suitable for horses, and most city flats simply aren't large enough. Keeping a horse at livery in the country or even in a city stable is often possible but it is usually terribly expensive and time-consuming to commute on a daily basis when job or school takes up most hours of your day. Don't feel that you must move to the country to do some riding. Most cities have reasonably good riding facilities within reach – by car if not by public transport – and you need only find out where they are and how to get there. Here, too, is where not owning a horse is an advantage. When the weather is bad or you are ill, you needn't make the trip to the horse. If it belongs to someone else, it won't need you to look after it or to feel guilty that it isn't being exercised. If the public stable near you isn't very good (see chapter 3 for some ways of analysing stables), look elsewhere. For a couple of years, five of my colleagues in publishing joined me in a car pool arrangement driving to a suburban riding school outside the city once a week after work;

in addition to expenses, we also shared friendly critical advice about our riding and lots of gossip about publishing.

If the main reason you don't own a horse is that you're not exactly sure just how deeply into riding you want to get, consider yourself sensible. Many beginners jump into horsekeeping as soon as they learn which side of the horse to mount on and too often they find themselves overburdened with responsibility. A number of the horse books written for beginners extol the joys of owning a 'back-garden' horse, but what the authors usually leave out is an accurate analysis of the money, time and effort involved. It *may* cost as little as £200 or £300 a year to maintain a horse, as the books put it, but a horse that becomes injured or ill can cost a great deal more than that and you won't even be able to ride. It's a wonderful experience to get to know an animal intimately, but you will quickly find out that familiarity can also breed contempt, especially when it means mucking out a box every freezing day in mid-winter when riding is impossible. Dedicated horse people learn to accept this as one of the realities of horse owning, but novices will often find their interest becoming weaker as the buckets of water become heavier.

If you restrict yourself to a lesson or two a week, you will be able to determine the extent of your interest more accurately than you would if Dobbin were a daily chore. If a small amount of riding doesn't seem to satisfy you, good. You'll probably make more of your occasional rides, learn more from them and find yourself progressing more rapidly.

Ambition and Ability – an Exercise in Self-Analysis

Now that we have made a virtue of not owning a horse, what next? What kind of a horseless rider are you going to become? Many people ride for simple enjoyment – getting out into the countryside, communicating with an animal or exercising in a pleasant way. Others ride because they love horses and want to be around them as much as possible. Several athletic people I know have gone into riding with the idea of mastering yet another sport – taking up the challenge of learning a new game with new rules (and new muscles) and experiencing the exhilaration that comes when one is capable of playing polo or making it around a hunt course. Excellence in riding for its own sake – because of its beauty and difficulty – appeals to many of us who thrill to watch an expert at work in the dressage ring or over huge fences in jumping classes. And there is the competitive element as well – the pride involved in carrying home a silver trophy for winning at a local horse trial.

Any and all of these ambitions are attainable for the horseless rider, even at the higher level, for many of our finest horsemen managed to make it to the top on the back of other people's horses. Although we may never get the chance to throw a leg over an Olympic jumper or to perform a levade aboard a Lippizaner, it is entirely possible for us to learn to show successfully, to go fox-hunting with the best packs in the country, to spend whole vacations on horseback or just a satisfying hour going around the ring at a fine stable, and to become horsemen in the process.

Learning to ride well enough to pursue our various goals is not, of course, a simple matter of checking the *Yellow Pages* for the closest stable and paying out a couple of pounds for an hour's worth of experience. On the other hand, you needn't go to the best instructor in the land and proclaim your intention to make the national equestrian team. (In addition to requiring a commitment of a few thousand pounds a year, the instructor would undoubtedly insist that he select a horse for you to buy.) But you *should* make the effort to learn the basics on the back of the most appropriate horse you can find under the supervision of the most appropriate teacher. Even if you have already progressed beyond the novice stage, you should consider taking lessons occasionally rather than just going out on your own. For one thing, you'll learn something and for another, you're likely to get yourself a more interesting horse. Not long ago, when I was taking lessons at a stable that did not offer hacking to the general public, my mother remarked: 'Haven't you learned how to ride *yet?*' I don't remember whether I explained that this was the only way I could ride at that stable or whether I pronounced loftily that even the best riders in the country never stop schooling themselves or their horses, but I do recall feeling rather pleased that I had reached the point where I knew I didn't know it all. Captain Alexis Podharjsky, former director of the Spanish Riding School in Vienna, wrote a book entitled *My Horses, My Teachers* about the animals that had taught him so much over the years. It seems that even after he graduated from the 'high school' of dressage, he continued to learn something from every new horse he mounted. 'Retrospectively,' he says, 'I realize that the constant endeavour to understand the creatures entrusted to my care became the reason why, though I was their trainer, I feel as their pupil today.'

As you spend more time on horseback, you will undoubtedly find that your ambitions will change as your ability increases. Each new horse you ride should open a door on to some aspect of riding or horsemanship and every experience ·will lead to another. I have known people who were convinced that trekking was the ultimate pleasure on horseback but who started setting up fences for the fun of it, only to find that the new ultimate pleasure then became cross-country jumping.

Attitude

As I've been implying, becoming a horseless rider involves first and foremost a question of attitude. An open mind is as important as natural ability and far more crucial than a fancy set of riding clothes. Before we get to the practical matters of what to wear, how to ride and where, let's consider for a moment that while you are analysing the prospective stable and horse, they will also be analysing *you*. So prepare yourself to make a good impression rather than one that will put you on the back of the least promising horse in the stable. How you ask your questions, how you act and what you wear may or may not be noticed, but it's worth taking the trouble to do things properly, just in case. You'll find that a certain degree of proficiency in these areas will add a great deal to your self-confidence, no matter what your level of expertise. So pay some attention to your manner and your speech when you approach a new stable for the first time. Don't, for heaven's sake, tell the owner that you can ride anything in the place. Answer all questions honestly, including the one about the amount of experience you have had. If you rode once seventeen years ago, don't tell anyone that you have ridden for seventeen years; the game will be up the moment you attempt to mount. On the other hand, if you have ridden every other day for the last year, don't be shy; tell the management that you are beyond the beginner stage and can handle the walk, trot and canter with confidence. And if you are subjected to an evaluation test or told you must have a guide accompany you, welcome the chance to prove yourself. This initial conversation is where vocabulary will count. But be careful using terms if you aren't really sure what you (or they) mean. Nothing sounds greener than a novice who demands a horse that can perform a piaffe just to show off; what shows is that you don't know much – yet.

If something puzzles you – or if you are anxious to learn, say, what the stablehand is doing to get that bridle in place – by all means ask questions. Don't be a pest (stablehands at busy stables don't often have a lot of spare time) but a good, thoughtful question and close attention to the answer will usually result in information. Whatever you do, please don't treat the stablehands or grooms like lowly servants. All too often I have seen renting riders (and even owners) act in a superior way to the people who muck out the stalls and clean the horses – this attitude is an unattractive one, to say the least. Keep in mind that the people who work around horses probably know more about horses than you do and certainly more about the charges in their care. Some stables and grooms have a policy not to allow amateurs to get involved in tacking up or down (for reasons of safety and efficiency), but if a stable seems shorthanded, it is never out of place to offer your help. You can learn a lot in the process and your co-operative attitude will be rewarded in kind. A rude person who insists that the 'help' give him or her a leg up and adjust the stirrups without politely asking for assistance is invariably going to arouse resentment. Tipping is not necessary except for special services beyond the call of duty (and, if you ride regularly at a stable, perhaps a Christmas gift might be in order), but common human decency is. After all, many grooms are doing their work because they love it and not just because they need the money. I recall one occasion when an older female rider behaved rather haughtily to the younger female stablehand who tacked up her horse, only to find the girl at her own dinner table the following evening. It turned out that the 'servant' and her daughter had been classmates at college!

Dress

Old clichés notwithstanding, clothes do not make the horseman, but they do help not only in terms of making a good impression and giving the rider a sense of self-confidence, but also in pure practical terms of comfort, safety and proficiency. Although riding clothes have become fashionable of late – blue jeans, Stetsons, boots and hacking jackets are as common in the city as they are at the stable – they were not designed for good looks alone. Each piece of riding apparel has been developed over the years for rather specific purposes – to be comfortable and long-wearing, and to assist the rider in maintaining a good, secure seat in the saddle. In the next chapter, I will briefly discuss the appropriate types of clothing for different styles of riding, and if you know that you are interested in one style and are committed enough to make the investment in proper apparel, go ahead and do so. But if you are unsure about what kind of riding you plan to do and don't know whether this will be the first of several rides or the last, your best bet is to wear simple, workaday clothes and to borrow some pieces of basic equipment for your first few times out.

Though you may end up investing in a pair of jodhpurs, breeches or riding boots, you'll be perfectly well dressed at the beginning in a plain pair of sturdy, well-fitting, well broken-in jeans and some kind of shoe or boot with a leather heel. Trousers should be snug at the knee and over the calf to prevent chafing (or 'strawberries'), which can be painful later on, but you may want the extra insurance of some seamless underwear or thin cotton tights beneath them to avoid discomfort in places where it matters. Flared trousers are not appropriate, but if that's all you have, put a rubber band or a bicycle clip on each leg to keep them from flapping. If your boots are low rather than mid-calf or knee-high, wear long socks. Avoid tennis shoes or shoes without a sturdy upper and a heel; being stepped on is painful and having your foot caught in a stirrup aboard a runaway is downright dangerous. In warm weather, a T-shirt or a jersey with short sleeves is perfectly acceptable; low-cut shirts or blouses look out of place on horseback and may result in painful sunburn. Equally out of place is long hair (on male or female) that is not put into pigtails or otherwise collected and confined. It may look romantic in advertisements for perfume or whatever to have a lass with flowing locks matching those of her horse ride off into the sunset, but that sort of romance doesn't mix very well with serious riding, Jewellery and heavy make-up are also inappropriate; the former is all too likely to be damaged and the latter will probably become covered with a noticeable layer of grime, but more important they indicate that the rider has something else on her mind than her horse. If you wear a jacket, make sure it is short enough so that it won't hang over your hips and see that the sleeves are generous enough to allow flexibility at the shoulder and elbow. Down waistcoats are practical in cold weather, since they give the arms great freedom; denim jackets that button at the waist are good so long as they are not too tight.

You should, of course, wear jodhpurs and jodhpur boots, or breeches and riding boots if you have them. But if you are a beginner or if you haven't already invested in these articles, don't race out to buy them. Wear well-fitting jeans and good shoes or boots with heels, and, after a lesson or two, ask your instructor for advice about clothing. There's no point in wearing out your best hunting outfit on a casual ride or a dusty session in the ring. Many people feel they will make a poor impression by not dressing to the teeth. I have two conflicting stories on that subject – so take your pick. Once, while I was visiting some friends in California, we decided to go riding at the local stable where no one in the party had been; on the chance that they might have a horse broken to an English saddle, I wore my breeches and boots and ended up with a relatively unschooled but lively and interesting horse. (It turns out that no one had asked for an English saddle or this horse in several weeks and so my ride was eventful, to say the least. The owners of the stable must have taken one look at my clothes and decided that I was Princess Anne.) But on another occasion, I tried the same tack at another stable, only to find that *their* tack was Western, and I was treated to a few embarrassing moments by having to hoist my smartened-up self into a down-to-earth stock saddle.

No matter what your basic gear is, however, you should have in your bag or car, or whatever it is you carry things in, a crop or a riding stick of some kind and a hard hat – the latter being especially important if you are a beginner and essential if you plan to do any jumping. Gloves are perfectly acceptable though not necessary, but if worn they should be made of a thin, supple material that will help (not hinder) your grip on the reins. Spurs, on the other hand, are to be avoided by the beginner or by riders mounting unfamiliar horses unless otherwise instructed. Spurs can be invaluable aids to the experienced rider but they are too often instruments of torture on untrained heels.

As soon as you are sure of yourself in the saddle you should get yourself some real riding apparel, since, as a horseless rider, you never know where your next horse will be taking you, whether it's to a fine private stable or into the show ring. Last-minute purchases or loans from friends for the sake of a special occasion may not be properly fitted or broken in, and you'll probably feel uncomfortable just when you want to be looking your best. If you are worried that the expensive clothes will be used only once a year check with your saddlery shop for used items, or think of the purchase as a potential hand-me-down for other members of the family or for friends. Stable bulletin boards are usually covered with advertisements for outgrown garments, so be sure to check there, too.

One accessory that is never mentioned in the horse books but that I have always found important regardless of where or whom I'm riding is a carrot, which I invariably steal from the refrigerator whenever I head for the stable. So while you are packing up your gear or getting yourself ready to meet the horse of your dreams (which for the horseless rider may be the next animal you ride), stick a carrot into your pocket and don't forget to use it after the ride is over. The stable management may not be impressed, but it will be appreciated by the equine recipient, even if he never lays eyes on you again.

Physical Considerations

One question that often arises when people set out to ride for the first time – in their lives or in the past few months – is 'How can I avoid getting sore?' Because soreness is one of the inevitable results of using muscles that have not been employed in some time. The degree of soreness depends, obviously, on the length of time you spend in the saddle and the type of riding you do, but some discomfort is probably in store, unless you take some precautions. I have already spoken about proper clothing that fits well and will help to prevent chafing sores, but what about those painful strains in the leg muscles, particularly in the thigh region? A person in good physical condition who exercises regularly by swimming or jogging may be using these muscles already and may experience little or no pain at all the day after spending an hour in the saddle. But if you do not exercise at all and would like to help loosen up those muscles before riding, you might try the exercises described in the box on page 30. For those of us who don't tend to plan ahead, the best precaution may simply be to get some Epsom salts or baking soda ready for a good long hot bath after your ride. You may still have some pain the day after you ride (or even on the second day following), but, like the hair of the dog in drinking liquor, there's nothing like another horseback ride to work off the muscle strain. Speaking of alcohol, by the way, you may find that a vigorous rubdown with alcohol will help to relieve your aches and pains. If you continue to ride on a regular basis, you will find that the pain will gradually disappear altogether.

George Morris, the dean of American trainers in forward-seat equitation, has only two exercises to recommend – standing on the balls of your feet on a step and pushing down on the heels to improve heel flexion and – perhaps more important – pushing away from the dinner table if you are inclined to be overweight. Like many experts, Morris believes that a fat rider is at a distinct disadvantage, and not just in the showring where appearance counts heavily, so to speak. A few pounds may not matter if you are able to develop a good seat in the saddle and can afford well-tailored riding clothes to hide your bulges, but no one, unless he or she is pretty weak or emaciated, can be too thin to ride. One look at top horsemen and women should be enough to curb the appetite! Remember, too, that riding is an athletic endeavour and that any athlete (equine as well as human) is better served by a trim physique, which will aid in achieving and maintaining balance, flexibility and skill. Slender thighs are more capable of holding their proper position to establish contact with the horse's sides, for example. Extra pounds of flesh that cannot be considered muscular are of little assistance to the rider and will add an unnecessary burden to the horse below.

Perhaps as important as weight and fitness is the mental attitude toward physical discipline – mind over matter, if you will. One problem that many beginning riders have, especially if they are beyond the age of innocence, is the awkwardness and resulting self-consciousness that comes with learning something new. Mentally we want to learn, but we may not be prepared to undergo the physical demands that the education involves. When one reaches an advanced level, it seems almost automatic and natural for one's legs, heels, hands, seat and head to move independently and yet in complete co-ordination, but for a beginner, many of these movements and positions will be totally unfamiliar. Keeping one's heels down, head up, eyes ahead, elbows at the side and hands both gentle and firm do not add up to the usual position that one maintains in an office or

If your family objects to your interest in riding, here are some arguments you can try.

1. *Don't tell me that riding is exercise. The horse does all the work!* Only a poor rider is a passenger on a horse. A good rider is constantly working to make the horse perform well. This is good mental exercise and it is excellent physical discipline as well. Why do you think they give Olympic medals to the riders instead of to the horses?

2. *Riding is dangerous and bad for your health.* Taking a fall can lead to injury, it's true, but skiing accidents are far more numerous and driving a car is even more dangerous. A good rider can learn how to prevent most accidents and to fall safely. Also, riding strengthens the lower-back muscles and is good preventive medicine for lower back problems which are common but not in those who ride regularly.

3. *Riding is cruel to animals.* A bad, abusive rider can be cruel to a horse, pulling on its mouth and running it ragged. But a good rider who understands equine mentality is good for a horse. Remember that modern-day saddle horses are domestic animals and will be far healthier and happier when trained properly than when they are allowed to run wild. An unruly, undisciplined horse can be a joy to watch in a field but he will never be handled or cared for very well. A good horse-and-rider team depends to a large extent on the willingness of the horse, not on the rider's ability to force it to go.

4. *You aren't strong enough to handle a horse.* No human is stronger than a full-grown horse, so we have developed ways of handling them that take brains and technique, not brute strength. This is why children and women often make better riders than men who rely on muscle to do the job.

5. *Horses aren't even as smart as pigs or dogs, so what's the challenge?* It's unfair to measure horse intelligence by the standards we use for other species. Horses are just as smart as they have to be for what they are. Your average 'dumb' hack knows a great deal more than most of its riders about how to get its own way – and that's a challenge right there. And when was the last time you tried to ride a pig anyway?

6. *Horseback riding is expensive and snobby.* True, it does take money to feed, equip and care for a horse, but riding once or twice a week is far less expensive than skiing or other sports involving an investment in equipment and facilities. As for snob value, horses aren't snobs and couldn't care less about the social or financial status of their riders so long as they ride well.

7. *Hacking is nice but hiking or jogging is better.* Jogging through the countryside may be better exercise, but for seeing the sights riding a horse is more rewarding. Shy animals are less frightened by a horse and rider than they are by a human on foot, and menacing dogs that can attack a runner will usually give up on a horse after barking a few times.

Riding Exercises

Becky Murrell, a physical therapist, has contrived some simple exercises for the horseman/horsewoman to train the muscles used in riding; they are especially useful for those interested in jumping but anyone who spends time in a saddle will find them helpful. Here are a few suggestions based on her techniques.

1. To help to keep your head and back straight and your shoulders well back, lie face down with your hands clasped behind your neck and a pillow under your abdomen. Raise your head, shoulders and elbows as high as possible and hold the position for a slow count of five.
2. To help you rise at the trot and to keep your knees in position, get down on your hands and knees and look up. Slowly raise one leg straight backwards. Lower, relax and repeat with the other leg.
3. To help to keep the inside of your knee and leg in contact with the saddle and to keep your toes pointing ahead rather than off to the side: sit in a firm chair with your feet flat on the floor. With your knees together and pointing straight ahead, lift your feet slightly off the floor and spread your ankles as far as they will go without separating your knees. Hold for a slow count of five and relax. Weights on each ankle will be useful if you wish to increase the strength of these muscles.
4. The hip abductors are the muscles that usually become sore in beginners, since they squeeze your knees together, but they are important for a strong seat in any rider. To strengthen them and help prevent soreness, sit in a chair with your knees apart and put a large beach ball between them. Squeeze your knees together as hard as you can for a slow count of ten.
5. For heel extension, you can use George Morris's exercise of standing on the balls of your feet on a step and pushing down on the heels. Or you can sit in a chair, raising your toes and feet toward the ceiling while your heels remain on the floor. You can make this exercise even more effective by adding a weight to the top of your feet.

around the house. It is very difficult at first to remember each of these components of the good 'seat' on a horse, especially if that animal is going at a gait faster than a walk. Simply keeping your balance and your wits about you is difficult enough.

I recall watching one lesson where an obvious beginner was having the usual problems learning to rise at the trot and was surprised that the instructor kept harping on the rider's heels rather than his hands which were flopping all over the place. Later, the instructor told me that there wasn't any point of getting the hands right until the legs (and the horse) were under control – so long as the horse's mouth wasn't being damaged.

Although it is embarrassing not to have your body under complete control and to look clumsy in the saddle, please keep in mind that everyone who rides has been through that awkward stage before you. Some people take to riding more quickly than others – you will often hear someone called a 'natural rider' – but no one achieves perfection or even a good imitation of it without some good, hard work. Steve Cauthen, the boy wonder, worked every day for nearly ten years before he became an 'overnight' sensation as a jockey, and though we may not have similar ambitions, we all want to become at least adequately proficient as riders, and that takes practice. It also takes a teacher, a stable and last but not least a horse – each of which will be discussed in the chapters that follow. Equally important, however, it takes a good attitude and a willingness to learn and to undergo the mental and physical discipline involved in learning.

I have asked several riding instructors and trainers how they evaluate new riders – on the basis of appearance, clothing, manners, vocabulary or attitude – and without exception each one of them told me that the *only* important requirement in a student was the last one on that list. The first four can be improved, cultivated or purchased, but the right attitude has to be there at the start and cannot be taught, no matter how good the teacher. With that in mind, let's look at some of the things that *can* be taught.

2
The Instructor

Anyone who has ever seen a Western film knows that riding is a pretty simple business – all you do is leap into the saddle, making sure that you end up facing the horse's head, grab the reins and kick like crazy with your spurs until the animal takes off, right? Wrong. Chances are that if you tried leaping into a saddle first time out, you'd end up on the ground on the other side of the horse. And that would only be the beginning of a fairly disastrous ride. Unlike cars, motorcycles or skateboards, horses are big, strong, living creatures with varying personalities and physical capabilities. Learning to handle, let alone master, such an animal takes knowledge, experience and skill on the part of the rider. Note that I didn't say strength. Horses will always be stronger than humans, but luckily we have a slight edge in the brain department and through centuries of trial and error have developed a number of effective ways of getting horses to do what we want. Since we have always wanted them to do different sorts of things – pulling carriages, carrying riders for long distances, charging enemies and showing off their beauty, speed or jumping ability – the methods of training have varied considerably. Although most people today use horses for pleasure riding, not all of those horses have been trained in the same way. Riders, too, are trained in different ways, or methods of equitation, depending on the horses they ride, the regions they live in and the types of riding they do.

A great many people ride horses without ever taking a lesson and some of them turn into perfectly good riders if they are persistent and have a degree of natural talent. But learning to ride without any prior knowledge or instruction is done primarily at the school of hard knocks and there are easier and far more effective ways for the beginner to learn the ABCs of riding than that. Before we head out on the road looking for the ideal stable and horse to ride, then, let's put the cart before the horse and discuss the types of instruction that are available and the ways to find them. Even before that, however, let's take a closer look at just what it is that the horseless rider needs to learn.

The Goals

In the United States, where I grew up, the horse world tends to divide itself into two general categories – 'Western' and 'English' – the former referring to the stock-seat equitation developed in the Western states by cowboys employed to herd cattle and the latter referring to all riding that does not involve the use of a Western saddle, even though those 'English' saddles might also be German, French, Italian or Argentine. Because the stock saddle, with its high horn in front and high cantle at the back, offers a secure seat even to the untrained rider, many people feel that lessons are unnecessary, and for the occasional Sunday rider this is probably true. As horseback riding has become increasingly popular, the Western style is no longer restricted to the western United States; in fact, it has found its way to 'dude ranches' all over the world, including even the New Forest in England and French vacation areas where tourists can be assured of a safe ride in a relatively comfortable saddle.

But any horseless rider serious enough to be reading this book must be prepared to deal with any riderless horse that happens to come along, and in Britain that horse is most likely to come equipped with something other than a Western saddle. 'English' saddles, of course, come in many different shapes and sizes, as a quick glance at any saddlery shop will reveal. There are all-purpose saddles for pleasure riding, jumping saddles of several kinds and dressage saddles, each one of them designed for a particular type of riding. I do not mean to imply that every opportunistic horseless rider needs to become expert in each of these specialities, but I do recommend a good, solid grounding in riding basics, which are best learned under the supervision of a riding instructor on the back of an experienced school horse. These basics are easily adapted, as we shall see, to more advanced forms of riding.

And what do these riding basics involve? Riding schools tend to organize courses of lessons according to beginning, intermediate and advanced stages of progress, and I believe that the horseless rider should – to take full advantage of the state of horselessness – achieve a degree of expertise somewhere beyond the beginner, though not necessarily in the advanced level. Specifically, one should learn how to control an average horse (leave the green, unschooled horse or the ill-mannered rogue to the experts for now) at the walk, trot (rising and sitting), canter and hand gallop. Handling the horse at these gaits is not enough, however; one must also be able to extend and collect the first three gaits and manage smooth transitions between them. One should know how to mount and dismount effortlessly, stop the horse when one wants, back up and make simple lateral and diagonal movements without losing one's balance or temper. The rider should be able to perform these various movements not only in a school or riding ring but also on the bridle path, either in a city park or in the open countryside. Because the occasional trail may offer a hazard or two, one must be prepared to deal with simple emergencies – a horse that shies, attempts to bolt, or becomes lame. And because that same trail may also offer an obstacle, such as a low wall, a fallen log or a stream, a lesson or two in jumping would not be a waste of time.

There are other important aspects of horsemanship that do not involve strict equitation – proper conduct while riding in company or across other people's property; a modicum of knowledge about horse care (how to tack and untack, how to lead a horse, clean out a hoof, how to determine whether a horse is ill, injured, or overworked, and so on). Much of this sort of information can be learned from books or simply from experience, but it is no less important than the ability to sit a horse well.

All of that sounds like a large order for the novice, but learning these things is not quite as demanding as, say, getting through medical school, so don't be discouraged before you start at the idea of taking lessons – even if you are well beyond the normal school age. Once the basic techniques have been mastered, you will need to practise as often as you can to improve your skills, but, happily, practising on horseback is one of the most pleasurable activities I know. You can always take a break from the work of concentrating on the placement of your heels or hands by taking a relaxing ride through the countryside, refreshing yourself and the horse, and discovering what all those lessons have really been for.

Many people beyond the beginner stage stop at the basics and never consider the idea of taking another lesson, but I find that most of these riders fail to get as much out of their occasional hacks as they could if they considered each ride a learning experience. When I started taking lessons after ten years of infrequent and casual rides, I found that my interest in horses quickly increased to the high pitch I had enjoyed at the age of fifteen. While I certainly advocate riding lessons for every beginner, I also recommend them for more experienced riders – not as a regular routine but as a useful way of increasing one's riding enjoyment. When you approach a new hacking stable and take a lesson rather than just hiring a horse, that stable will be able to evaluate your expertise quickly and trust you with a better horse the next time. Many good stables do not offer hacking at all so that the only way to ride there is to take instruction. Once, whilst visiting my parents at a resort area, I went in to the local stable to inquire about riding. The bridlepath rides that were available involved only walking and trotting because they catered primarily for novice tourists, but there was a lesson programme as well. So I signed up for a class and within half an hour I was cantering around the instructor picking up a few pointers about a type of equitation in which I had never been schooled. The next morning, when I came back, the stable manager offered me a good horse and allowed me to ride by myself, since he knew I could handle the animal.

The Types of Equitation

Since this is not an instruction manual and since any instructor has his or her own methods for teaching equitation, this section is designed only as a superficial guide for the horseless rider, a brief look at the different styles of riding that are popular today, and a hint or two for the rider who finds him- or herself riding an unfamiliar horse who may not have been to the same riding school as you have.

Balanced-seat Equitation

The above is a relatively new term for a very old form of riding, one that riders all over the world have been using for years, perhaps without giving it a name. The easiest way for me to describe the balanced seat is to ask you to picture someone riding bareback, without the benefit of any special saddle to keep his weight forwards or backwards, and without stirrups to regulate the extension of his legs. As anyone who has ever ridden bareback knows, balance is what keeps you aboard – not the reassuring presence of a leather seat or a set of stirrups to help you rise at the trot. On a malnourished or tiny horse, one can (maybe) stay in place by holding the animal in a death grip with one's legs, but on a normal horse, the rider's legs must be in the right place (directly below the shoulder-to-hip line); the seat must be deep and over the horse's centre of gravity; and the hands must work independently rather than being used to hang on, which will only jab the horse painfully in the mouth. At any gait faster than the walk, the rider must remain in perfect synchrony with the horse's rhythm – neither ahead nor behind – if he is to remain on the horse's back, and the legs must be free not to grip but to regulate the horse's speed by giving and relieving pressure against its sides. (This involves keeping the heels down, incidentally, as in a saddle so that the calves may be kept in constant contact with the horse's sides for impulsion. Keeping the toes pointed down may seem more natural or more secure, but the rider is actually in a poor position to maintain control.)

Because this book is addressed to the rider who is committed to riding but not to one particular animal trained to one particular method, I recommend the balanced seat as the most adaptable of styles and – to many experts – the most effective. Whether you are to become interested in dressage, open jumping or distance riding, the balanced seat is the most useful basic approach. One can learn it in any kind of saddle, on a school horse or a fine privately owned purebred, even one that has been trained to a special style.

Although many instructors may not even know what you mean by the expression 'balanced seat', you will probably find that most of them – if they are not exclusively committed to forward-seat equitation – are teaching at least some variation of this style. The rider's seat is well into the saddle, the back is straight (at all gaits, except the gallop and over jumps), the legs are on a line with the back, and the hands are neither resting on the withers below the horse's head nor carried higher than the crest of the neck.

Most people who jump horses feel that the forward seat is the only way to make a horse do so effectively, by keeping one's weight forward and off the animal's back, freeing the hindquarters to do their stuff. This is all well and good for the trained hunter who is willing and experienced and needs little encouragement to take a fence. (The two-point seat – meaning contact only with the legs not the seat bones – is used even by balanced seat riders at the gallop and during a jump after take-off.) But when one is trying to jump an unwilling horse that is hard to control, most trainers will agree that a secure seat in the saddle with one's weight back rather than forwards will give more impulsion, more control and more safety for the rider. Just as it is effective to lean back rather than forward when a horse disobeys, so it is more effective when one is asking a horse to jump to make sure that one has control of the rear-end 'engine'. It is a rule of every horseman's thumb to correct a horse by moving forward (not stopping) and it is only by keeping one's legs and seat in the position of control that one can keep the horse going. (Another useful rule to remember is that a rider has very little control when out of the saddle – either over the withers or on the ground!) Experienced riders can maintain strong control with their legs alone, but until you reach that stage, your seat is an essential adjunct to your legs.

At a horse show some day, watch the major show jumping classes, especially the horses that are obviously excited and difficult to ride. The riders do not resemble those in the hunter classes, for they are back in the saddle until the point of take-off, keeping as much control and forcing as much impulsion as possible. Steeplechase or cross-country riders also stay back, especially if the take-off is anything less than perfect, for it is important that they remain in the saddle – not just to win but to stay in one piece. School horses are not comparable to the brilliant open jumpers capable of leaping six-foot fences or to the steeplechasers who can clear five feet going thirty miles an hour, but the principle is the same: for success the rider can't afford to let the horse take charge of the situation.

Perhaps the best expert to watch for a real understanding of the balanced seat is a dressage rider, for it is out of dressage techniques that the balanced seat developed. 'Dressage' is a French word meaning 'training' or 'schooling' and in horsemanship it means that the horse is taught to be supple, balanced, obedient and cadenced. A well-schooled dressage horse in motion is a thing of beauty, moving rhythmically and with spirit yet perfectly under the control of the rider, whose aids are so subtle they are virtually invisible. (See page 41 for a more complete description of dressage.)

Forward-seat Equitation

Although this is a very popular style of riding today, it is, perhaps surprisingly, the most recent in its development. Unlike other styles, the forward seat was not developed for comfort during long hours in the saddle, so important in the good old carless, trainless days. It was devised as the most efficient method of enabling a horse to perform certain short-term but intensive activities – racing at full speed and jumping over obstacles. For these relatively extreme movements, a horse needs as much freedom as possible to move its head and neck

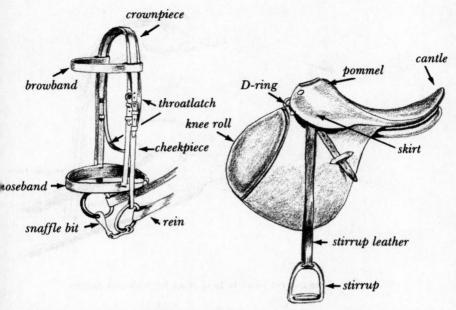

What the well-dressed horse will be wearing at a stable that offers forward-seat equitation: a snaffle bridle and a jumping saddle

(essential to balance) and its hindquarters (essential for power). Thus, the rider, helped by the design of the saddle, remains forward in position at speed and in the air over a jump, keeping as little weight as possible on the hindquarters and giving freedom to the forequarters. The construction of the forward-seat saddle is, therefore, very different from those we have met so far: a relatively high cantle to keep weight from slipping back, and a knee roll to give security and a steady position to the legs, which are, in this style of riding, the main source of control, since the seat is often a two-point rather than a deep three-point position. Stirrups are short to relieve the horse of the rider's weight – more so in race riding and less so in cross-country riding over jumps where security and control are more important than speed.

In addition to a special saddle, the average horse trained as a hunter will probably also wear a running or standing martingale, a piece of tack designed to keep the horse's head

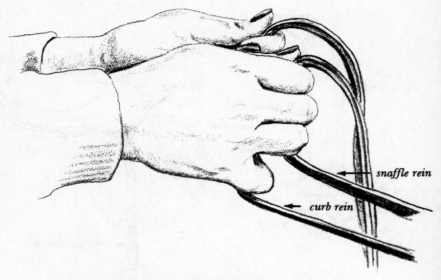

snaffle rein

curb rein

One of the correct ways to hold reins for a double bridle

relatively low, to prevent it from rising too high and thus interfering with balance (and also with the rider's face, which is closer to the horse's neck than in other styles). Although there are always exceptions, most hunter-trained horses also wear snaffle bits rather than double bridles, which tend to force a high head carriage, though on jumpers it is not surprising these days to see any number of different bits, including the Western hackamore.

Most hunters and jumpers are thoroughbreds or part-thoroughbreds, long-bodied and long-limbed, with gaits that are less collected than those of the high-stepping, collected breeds (and nonbreeds). These animals, because of the refinement of their breeding, are rarely found in hacking stables and their willingness to move ahead rarely requires the constant encouragement that the usual school horse demands if one wants anything more than a slow trot. Nevertheless, even the occasional rider may be given a chance to ride a hunter type, and it is worth learning how this is done, just in case.

If your instructor does not know the fine points (or even the rough ones) of forward-seat equitation, you can, by watching

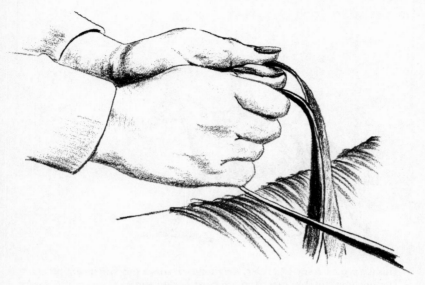
One way to hold snaffle reins

hunter classes at horse shows, gather important tips. Observe how the riders sit on their animals, adjusting the length of strides between jumps; keeping their balance directly over the withers rather than over the horse's back; and tilting forwards once the horse has taken off for a jump, keeping contact with the horse's mouth yet allowing the horse freedom to extend its neck as it jumps.

Dressage

We have covered the two basic riding styles most commonly practised and taught these days, but there are, of course, many other types of riding that are worth exploring by the horseless rider who may suddenly find himself confronted with a riding offer that is just too good to refuse. Some of these will be dealt with later on, but because dressage comes out of the classic tradition of horsemanship that has been written about by experts from Xenophon to Podhajsky, and because instruction in dressage is offered at many schools and stables as part of the education of every well-rounded horseman, it deserves special attention here.

This is a typical hunt-seat rider, weight forward over the withers at the canter. The horse is suitably tacked in a forward-seat saddle, single-reined snaffle bridle and a running martingale to keep the horse from throwing its head and evading the bit. The rider wears a hard hat, jacket, breeches and riding boots

Dressage is familiar to anyone who has seen the 'high school' horses of the Spanish Riding School perform their airs above the ground or who has watched a dressage test, either on its own or as part of the three-day or combined training events that Princess Anne, for one, has made television-worthy. At first glance, a dressage rider may seem to be doing nothing at all and one tends to admire the brilliantly trained horse performing subtle and intricate moves without a cue. Actually, dressage is an expression of perfect co-operation between horse and rider, the result of long hours of practice. Because the rider must have a deep, secure seat and an erect upper body, the stirrups are long and the saddle balanced in the middle of the horse's back (not forward as on the hunter or back as on the saddle horse). This position gives the rider complete control with both seat and legs so that only the slightest pressure or movement will indicate to the horse that a new movement is requested. The bridle is usually a double-bitted one, to ensure a high head carriage and perfect collection. Ideally, the dressage horse is always on the bit (completely under the rider's control and responsive to every move of the hands, seat or leg) and prepared to respond to whatever command may be given.

Dressage should not, however, be relegated to an elevated category of riding in which only a few may participate. Indeed, dressage has a great deal to offer even the most ordinary of horses and riders, for its basics are neither difficult to understand nor difficult to learn. I have often been surprised to find that the dowdiest looking hack and school horses are familiar with certain dressage movements – the half pass, simple two-tracking or leg yields, and turns on the haunches (see glossary on page 62). These movements may not be performed well – it often takes some doing to push the right buttons, in fact – but it is always a wonderful feeling to find out that you and the horse have something in common, an appreciation for a motion that is neither straight ahead nor back, but sideways or around. These lateral movements are invaluable in teaching the horse to be supple and obedient, but they are also useful to know when a gate needs closing, a jacket needs to be hung on a fence, or a move needs to be made to the side without involving a complete turn. Manoeuvrability is always important on the trail, in the ring or approaching a fence, and the horse that can be manoeuvred without dismounting is always worth rewarding. Collection and extension and bending on turns are part of all styles of riding, but they are the essence of dressage and a horse whose gaits can be 'rated' (speeded up or slowed down) without breaking stride is a useful animal indeed.

There are, of course, many other forms of riding – side-saddle, racing, Western stock-saddle equitation and so on, but these will be dealt with in chapter 8 as sidelines for the adventurous rider to explore. In this chapter, I have tried to stick to the basics as you find them in the horse books, at horse shows and in lesson programmes at riding stables. In many parts of the country you may not have a choice about the type of instruction offered or the way in which your horse-of-the-hour has been trained. The point is that, for the horseless rider, any style is suitable at the beginning so long as you develop

A classic dressage seat at the extended (long-strided) trot. Note how other styles of riding have adapted certain elements of this fine, traditional form of equitation

confidence in the saddle (and out of it) and any horse is acceptable so long as you have that confidence and some idea of what to expect. If you are one of those fortunates who has complete access to a single animal owned but unused by someone else, you can afford to specialize, but most of us must make do with various horses or with a horse ridden by various riders, and that calls for a generalist's approach. I am delighted to report that every horseman and horsewoman I have met or read about can be typed as a generalist – capable of handling any equine that comes along regardless of experience or temperament. And so, to make our attitudes and ability as flexible as our riding muscles, let's apply to one of those generalists for some advice and instruction.

Formal Instruction

Selecting a potential instructor can be as complicated and difficult as picking a family doctor, since a good personal relationship is almost as important as actual expertise. Someone who screams at a rider who takes criticism badly is probably not going to be able to teach much, while some riders can't learn anything unless instruction is delivered in the most forceful way. Many beginners need a good deal of reassurance, an instructor who builds a sense of self-confidence by progressing slowly on one or a series of well-schooled, well-mannered horses. More experienced but timid riders need encouragement and support to go beyond the basics to more demanding aspects of the sport, such as jumping, riding competitively or simply getting onto more difficult horses.

You needn't like the person who is giving you a lesson, but you should respect him or her and be willing to handle criticism, since there will be some. There's no point in taking a lesson unless you plan to learn something, even if it goes against what you have been taught previously. If that arises, you should feel free to ask the reasons behind a particular piece of instruction – not by presenting a counter-argument but simply by asking for an explanation. At one point in my chequered career, I overlapped lesson programmes at two different stables, one where I was being taught the balanced seat on average school horses and another where I was learning forward-seat equitation on a private horse. The former instructor insisted that I sit straight-backed with my weight in the centre of the saddle, while the latter kept trying to make me sit forward and use only my legs (not my seat bones) to move the horse forward. I was quite confused at first, but I eventually learned that each method has its reasons: the school horses needed the extra push and the private horse did not; the former instructor wanted to emphasize dressage movements and the latter wanted to prepare me for jumping. Thanks to the willingness of both teachers to explain the different horses and the different goals, I was soon able to sort it all out.

It goes without saying that riding instructors should know a great deal about horses and horsemanship, but for most students, an instructor should be a good teacher first and an expert rider second. It's very impressive to be able to tell your friends that your teacher was a former member of the national Equestrian Team, but it doesn't do you much good if you can't understand a word he says or if he can't articulate his techniques. Many instructors fall into habits of using phrases, which they can no longer define in plain English; the glossary on page 56 is intended to help the confused rider, but if you're really having trouble, it might be a good idea to find another instructor.

But before we look for another instructor, how do we go about finding the first one? The initial step, of course, is deciding just what it is you want to learn. It would be a waste of time learning to ride a dressage horse when you'd rather be able to handle a hunter. (Actually, for the horseless rider, nothing is a waste of time; sooner or later, you'll want to be able to take advantage of any and every riding situation that crops up!) Once you have selected the style that suits you, you must find a stable where instruction is available. Obviously a stable that specializes in pleasure riding is more likely to have lessons in that than in jumping, but many stables have more than one teacher while others have none at all.

The least reliable way of finding good instruction is the *Yellow Pages*, but if you are unfamiliar with stables in your area, this may be the most convenient way of finding out which local stables offer instruction (or claim that they do). A telephone call will ascertain what kind of lessons are available, whether there is room for you, and what the time and financial arrangements will be. An on-the-spot evaluation is much more effective, however, than a conversation over the telephone, so arrive a few minutes before your scheduled lesson and have a look around the stable and at any lessons in progress to see whether the investment will be worthwhile. (See chapter 3 for advice about finding and analysing stables.)

A better way of finding a good teacher – and getting yourself a good introduction – is to ask a friend who rides for a recommendation. If that friend is a valued client, the instructor will probably welcome you with a special personal touch, and you will have the advantage of knowing beforehand just what to expect from the stable, the horses and the teacher – as well as what will be expected of you.

Another good way of selecting a riding teacher is to visit a horse show and watch the competition – especially the equitation classes for both youngsters and adults in which riders rather than horses are being judged. Look at the winners and ask around for their coaches or teachers (who can usually be found hanging over the rail or at the ingate giving their pupils lavish praise or constructive criticism). Approach an instructor by congratulating him or her on the pupil's achievement and ask whether he or she might be willing to take on another pupil – i.e., yourself. If you are a beginner or can afford the time and money for a weekly lesson only, a successful teacher involved in preparing youngsters or training young horses for top-level competition may not even be interested in your custom, but don't be put off by a refusal. Ask the instructor to recommend an assistant or a protégé who could take you on. You needn't be a pest – after all, the instructor has students to coach at the show – but if you show sufficient polite enthusiasm and interest you should be able to get some helpful tips.

The most reliable way of finding good riding instruction, however, is to consult the British Horse Society (care of the National Equestrian Centre, Kenilworth, Warwickshire, CV8 2LR) for a list of approved riding establishments. Their useful, annually published booklet, *Where to Ride* (available for £1.50 at the time of writing), gives a list of all riding schools approved and recognized by the Society, which is the national organization responsible for equitation and the promotion and encouragement of the welfare of horses and ponies. The BHS was formed in 1947 and represents the interests of the average rider and of riding schools, which it inspects on a regular basis. More appropriate for this chapter, the Society holds examinations every year for instructors, and awards Instructor and Assistant Instructor Certificates to qualified riding teachers. Although there are many good riding schools in Britain that do not, for one reason or another, appear on the BHS approved list and although there are good instructors who do not have BHS certificates, the novice can be assured of qualified instruction in a suitable school on suitable school horses by using the Society's approved list as a guide. In addition to listing the riding establishments by area, the booklet gives specific information about the number of horses, the names of instructors, the school's particular specialities and facilities and other pertinent details.

If you would prefer to get your instruction stage over with in one intensive swoop, rather than learning in weekly lessons for several weeks or months, you should look into the possibility of equestrian centres or establishments with resident programmes. These exist throughout the British Isles and, for a price, you can learn an enormous amount in a very short time, stable management as well as equitation.

Once you have selected an instructor, you should ask for advice about how to approach your equestrian education. Should you have private lessons – forever, or only at the beginning? Would you do well in a group, and if so how many people would that involve? Or perhaps a semi-private lesson, with one or two other riders, would give you the most attention for your money. (I tend to believe that groups of more than six are usually worthless and that private lessons are important only for the first few beginning lessons.) If you have your heart set on a group lesson with a friend or two who may be riding at a more advanced level, don't complain but do what the instructor suggests, so long as it is within reason. You'll learn more if you ride at your own level for a while, progressing at your own pace rather than at someone else's. With concentration and practice on your part, you'll soon catch up with your friends. If you must rely on your friends for a car pool, for instance, explain the situation to your instructor, who will probably try to work out a convenient lesson arrangement.

Courses of lessons, prices, personalities and the quality of school horses will vary considerably from one stable to the next, so you must be realistic about what you can afford and what you really want. No instructor is likely to be perfect in fulfilling all of your requirements, so you must judge for yourself which ones you are willing to sacrifice or compromise on. You may find that you will learn a great deal more in a very expensive half hour with the best coach in town than you will in a cheaper group lesson where you have to share the teacher with ten other riders. You may find that five lessons a week on a sour school horse gives you less than a weekly hour on a beautifully athletic, private animal. Or you may find that the exact opposite is true, as I have on a number of occasions. I remember almost every word spoken by a fine instructor who taught at a huge public stable that required him to teach as many as twelve students at a time on average school horses. In fact, I feel that every lesson I had there, cheap as they were, was worth far more than lessons costing twice as much at fancier stables where the owners were far more interested in selling me an expensive thoroughbred than in teaching me to jump a crossrail. When you are starting out, a well-schooled 'push button' horse that does everything you ask (even if you don't ask correctly) can give you a good ride and some self-confidence, but after you have learned the basics, a difficult or sour horse is almost guaranteed to teach you more. And if you're paying for instruction over and above the price of a hack, that's the horse you need.

Informal Instruction

If you can afford only one lesson a week, say, and you have reached the level where you can hire a horse to take out alone, there are several ways in which you can supplement your education by working on your own. Doing homework in this way will be successful only if you know what you are practising, however, so ask your instructor at the end of each lesson what you can do for yourself without supervision. You can work on riding without stirrups, for instance, to improve your seat and balance, or you can practise collecting and extending the horse at different gaits, even on a pleasure ride. If you have access to a school, work on more controlled exercises, such as any dressage movements you may be learning or the basic application of aids in asking for changes of gait, correct leads at the canter and so forth. (See page 60 for more suggestions.)

If your problem is that your legs tend to move forward or flop around rather than stay in the proper place, or if your heels slide up rather than down, you may need someone to watch you if you don't have a mirror to ride in front of so that you can give yourself an occasional check. But that someone needn't be your instructor; anyone who knows what to look for can help you here, and you can offer to help in return by watching for your friend's particular faults. I have often learned something while riding in company with better riders, listening to their comments when I asked for advice about particular problems encountered along the way. Not long ago, I rode in a city park and it was very helpful indeed to have an experienced friend along to tell me how to handle a horse that believed he was being attacked by joggers and nannies pushing prams. Guides on trail rides or treks can be good sources of information, even if their primary function is to make sure that no one gets lost rather than to improve your riding technique. Don't interrupt when the lead rider is busy reassuring a novice or making sure that everyone is aware of low-hanging branches ahead, but do take advantage of quiet moments to ask a question or two about the way he rides or about the way in which your horse may have been trained.

Remember, though, if you are asking for criticism without paying for it, to take it in the proper spirit. Don't resent a helpful remark; if it is helpful, be grateful, and if you feel it is uncalled for, thank the criticizer for the effort and do what you think is best. Even in a situation where you feel that you know more than the instructor or trail guide, keep an open mind and a closed mouth. You'll learn something – a new trail, a horse's particular habits or whatever – and you can always demonstrate your own knowledge by riding as well as you know how rather than by talking about it. (If you feel the need to instruct, read on to chapter 9 about ways to earn extra money or free rides by becoming a teacher yourself.) The only time that I've found it necessary to speak up is when a horse is being abused by someone thoughtless or inexpert enough to cause needless pain or confusion. In such a case, you can adopt a relatively mild approach ('Aren't you scaring Horace?') or a firm one ('Please don't hold the reins so tight; you're hurting his mouth!') depending on the abuser, but do adopt *some* manner to avoid suffering, both equine and human. My only caution here is that you make sure that abuse is being committed; many expert horsemen use methods that may seem cruel to the novice but that are necessary if the horse is to become obedient. Whips, spurs and severe bits are definitely harmful in the wrong hands, but they can be effective tools when applied by a horseman. The best way to learn the difference is to watch an expert at work, and this involves perfecting the technique of observation, whether or not you are paying for the privilege.

If, for instance, you take an occasional lesson, you'd be wasting your money if you arrived a few minutes before the lesson and left immediately afterwards. One thing that every horseless rider must learn how to do is hang around – keeping your eyes and ears open the whole time. Watch other lessons in progress, observing the riders and listening to what the instructor tells them. You may not learn much from an 'up-down' class in which beginners are learning to rise at the trot, but you'll pick up valuable tips from more advanced classes. If no lessons are in progress, you can watch trainers schooling private horses, asking them any questions you have when the schooling session is over. Park yourself next to an instructor or a trainer at a horse show and ask him to comment on individual riding styles. If a rider uses a different technique from yours, or a special piece of tack with which you are unfamiliar, don't hesitate to ask someone who knows what it's all about. If a horse makes a mistake or if a rider you picked out as the best doesn't win, try to find out the reasons.

Another virtue in hanging around is that you can't help but learn something about horse care and stable management. If the instructor or the stable help allows it, ask if you may tack or untack the horse you have been assigned. If you don't know how to put a bridle on, watch it being done and then try it yourself. Make mental notes of grooming methods and techniques, and learn what the different pieces of equipment are designed to do. Offer to help by grooming, mucking out, lugging bales of hay or whatever needs doing. Walking a horse to cool it out, helping another rider to mount and adjusting his stirrups or just remaining interested but out of the way will help convince the stable people that you are serious and considerate. The more time you can manage to spend being useful around a stable, the more you will be welcomed and the more you will learn.

Book Learning

During all those hours that you don't spend in the saddle or hanging around the stable, you can feed your hunger for equestrian knowledge by reading books and looking at the pictures. Here and there in this book I mention a few titles that are worth their weight in information, and below are listed some books on the different riding styles. But before you race out to your bookshop or library to stock up, ask your instructor to recommend books that will supplement what he or she has been trying to teach you.

Since I have spent most of my adult life in the book-publishing business, I tend to collect books, read them and trust what they say. So when I started riding seriously after a ten-year hiatus, I naturally sought the best books on the subject. One publishing colleague, an excellent rider, told me that the finest book around was Waldemar Seunig's *Horsemanship* (Robert Hale) and it quickly ended up on my bedside table. A fine book it is, but at that point in my education, it was more than I could handle, especially the part where Seunig, in the tradition of his place and time (Germany in the 1950s) described the configuration of the ideal rider, dismissing the endomorph (heavy-set) and mesomorph (medium build) in favour of the ectomorph (thin). Since I was definitely an endomorphic type then, I was nearly convinced to give up equitation for crochet, but luckily my instructor intervened and sent me in the direction of Mr Right – in this case Gordon Wright, author of *Learning to Ride, Hunt, and Show*, which is aimed at the novice rather than the sophisticated expert.

In spite of my bias for books, I must admit that reading may not be the most valuable way for the horseless rider to learn (with the exception of reading this book, of course). Books on equitation and training are very instructive and useful, but only if you are able to apply those written lessons to daily work, which usually involves having your own horse. Many instructors have their own methods of teaching and may be annoyed if they feel you are trying to outguess them by learning contradictory methods or if you get too far ahead of yourself by trying to understand technical matters beyond your ability. The most frustrating books for horseless readers, of course, are those devoted to horsekeeping. I call these 'wish books' and I collect them anyway, in preparation for the morning I find that pony tied up in the garden, and I study everything in them just because I find everything about horses and horse care of great interest. The most useful books, however, and this includes some of the magazines as well, are those written by experts in the field who enjoy sharing their own experiences as well as their knowledge.

Membership of the British Horse Society, incidentally, entitles one for a nominal sum (£7 yearly for a full member, £3.50 for a junior or associate member) not only to join 25,000 like-minded horse people but to enjoy various privileges, including a broad selection of books, booklets and films made available at reasonable prices.

The points of a horse and rider

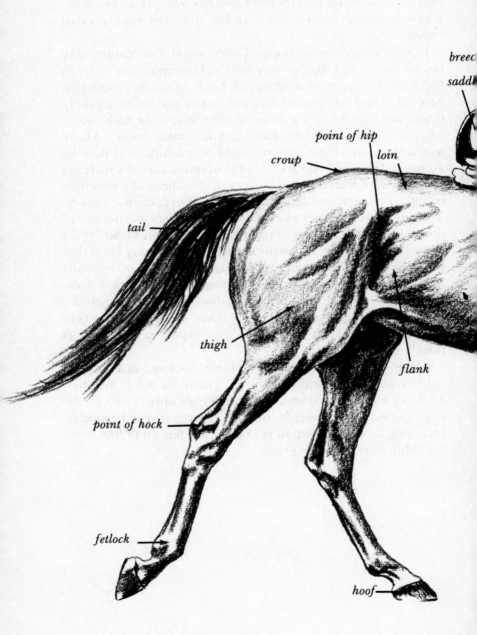

hun

breec

saddl

point of hip

loin

croup

tail

point of hock

thigh

flank

fetlock

hoof

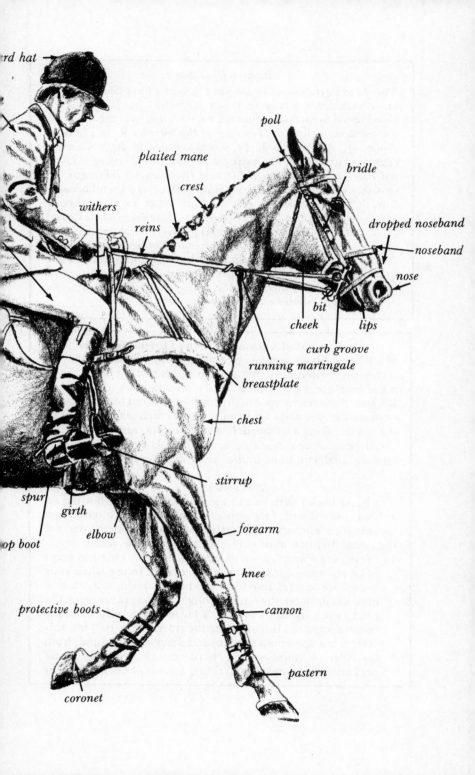

rd hat

poll

plaited mane

bridle

crest

withers

reins

dropped noseband

noseband

nose

bit

cheek

lips

curb groove

running martingale

breastplate

chest

stirrup

spur

girth

elbow

forearm

op boot

knee

protective boots

cannon

pastern

coronet

Books on Equitation

Two good introductory books are J. Licart's *Basic Equitation* and H. Wynmalen's *Equitation* (both published by J. A. Allen). Good books on dressage abound, each with its own theories, but the most accessible are *Dressage for Beginners* by R. L. Ffrench-Blake (J. A. Allen), J. Froissard's *Guide to Basic Dressage* (Pelham) and Alois Podhajsky's *The Complete Training of Horse and Rider in the Principles of Classical Horsemanship* (Harrap). A. Crossley's *Training Your Horse* (Stanley Paul) is a useful book to consult for ideas about reschooling. Other excellent books worth owning are Lt. A. L. D'Endrody's *Give Your Horse a Chance* (J. A. Allen), W. Museler's *Riding Logic* (Eyre Methuen) and my old favourite *Horsemanship* by Waldemar Seunig (Robert Hale).

There are many horse magazines, but if you want the journal that offers the most for all aspects of equitation, I recommend *Horse and Hound*. Others include *Riding, Light Horse* and *Stable Management* (available only on subscription).

An Annotated Glossary for the Horseless Rider

Most horse books contain glossaries – one-line definitions of rather mysterious horsy terms that appear in the back of the book and are rarely given much attention by the reader. Because these terms are usually meaningless out of context and because the glossaries are usually out of reach when you are in the saddle taking a lesson, here are a few terms and phrases that you'll hear around a stable or in the school that are worth reading, understanding and committing to memory.

Points of the Horse

Any horse book worth its salt block has a diagram showing an animal covered with tiny arrows, each one giving a name to a specific area. The terms defined below, however, refer to parts of the horse that one must care about while in the saddle.

1. *Mouth*, as in 'keep your hands off his mouth'. This may seem to be an odd expression for an instructor to use when your hands are several feet from the horse's head, but what is meant is to loosen the reins slightly to put less pressure on the bit, to use a lighter 'contact'. A horse with a 'soft' mouth is responsive to the bit, allowing the rider to control him; this animal is a horseman's dream and deserves light hands from his rider. A horse with a 'hard' mouth – usually found around hacking stables and riding schools – tries to evade the

bit in order to control the rider, who will probably try to apply more pressure, creating in turn even more resistance on the part of the horse. This horse should probably be reschooled or fitted with a different bit if he is to be ridden successfully.

2. *Poll*, as in 'flex at the poll'. This word refers to the area just behind the horse's ears, the point where the horseman wants his horse to flex, thereby lowering his head somewhat indicating that he has accepted the bit, or is 'on the bit', ready to do whatever the rider wants.

3. *Forehand*, as in 'heavy on the forehand'. This has nothing to do with the horse's tennis game, but refers to the front half of the animal (specifically shoulder and forelegs). Since a horse's 'motor' is in his hindquarters, a horse who is heavy on the forehand tends to be a bit out of balance and tends to pull on the reins, forcing the rider forward. This tendency is acceptable in some horses (those who pull vehicles, run races, etc) but not in jumpers, for instance, where the impulsion – or power – must come from behind if the animal is to be able to leap a fence or stop and turn on a sixpence. A horse who performs a 'turn on the forehand' is making a 180-degree turn in place, keeping his forelegs in place and moving his hindquarters around.

4. *Withers*, as in 'keep your hands down by (or above) his withers'. This word refers to the top of the shoulder joint just in front of the saddle. A horse's height is measured from the withers to the ground – not in inches but in 'hands' (equivalent to four inches). A horse that stands 60 inches high at the withers is therefore referred to as a 15-hand horse. Some horses have low withers, which are comfortable for bareback riding but sometimes incapable of keeping a saddle in place, necessitating the use of a breastplate. Horses with wide or high withers may require a special saddle or pad to prevent saddle sores from constant pressure and rubbing. If you hold the reins too far above or below the withers, you may find that your hands are not able to control the bit effectively or indeed the horse itself.

5. *Girth*, as in 'put your foot behind the girth'. This refers to the area of the horse below the saddle where the girth can be touched by the rider's foot. A schooled horse will respond to pressure at or behind the girth in different ways – taking the former as a sign to move ahead and the latter as a sign to keep his hindquarters from swinging out to the side.

6. *Near side*, as in 'mount on the near side'. This is the left side of the horse, from which a horse is always led, mounted and dismounted. (The right side is the off side.) This tradition, which is nearly universal today, once had a practical purpose – to keep the rider's sword, which was suspended from his left side, from swinging over the animal as he mounted or dismounted.

7. *Inside*, as in 'inside rein' or 'inside leg'. When a horse is moving (or bending) around a turn, the inside is the side of the animal closer to the direction in which he is moving; the outside is the other side, or, in a ring, the one that faces the outer edge of the ring. If you are moving around a ring to the left, the right side of the horse is the outside. During the counterclockwise trot, one rises on the left diagonal (moving up as the horse's right or outside leg moves forward), and during the counterclockwise canter the horse should be on the left lead, which means that the left leg is the leading leg.

8. *Hindquarters* or *haunches*. This is the origin of the horse's moving power or impulsion and is the area that the rider controls with his legs and seat. Many horsemen can successfully control a horse using no reins, indicating that to the rider the most important part of the horse is the hind end. A turn on the haunches is a 180-degree turn in place in which the hindquarters remain still and the forelegs move around.

9. *Hocks*, as in 'keep his hocks under him'. This refers to the part of the hind leg comparable to the human heel; when the hocks are under the horse, this means that the horse is moving forward properly, springing from his hind legs rather than pulling himself with his forelegs.

Points of the Rider

Few instruction books have diagrams of the human figure with little arrows defining parts of the rider, but these are no less important to successful riding than points of the horse.

1. *Hands*, as in 'light' hands. Many beginners assume that the horse is controlled with the reins and that a good pair of hands must be strong. Since a horse is far stronger than a person and since a hired horse is usually smarter in the use of the bit, the use of force on the reins can only lead to trouble unless properly applied. If a horse is not on the bit, the reins are virtually useless and the horse must be outsmarted if control is to be regained. This may involve a quick jab with the reins, not steady pressure, but it also involves getting control of the

hindquarters and other methods too complicated to describe here. The point is that light hands, applying pressure properly and only when necessary, are far more effective than heavy hands, which have ruined many a good horse with a soft mouth.

2. *Eyes*. Since the name of the game in riding is balance and since one's balance can be affected by even the turn of a head, you should always keep your eyes up and in the direction you wish the horse to move. If your eyes are down, your head is down and your weight too far forward; if you are looking to the left and wish to move straight, you may be confusing your horse.

3. *Elbows*. These are of very little use to the rider unless they are at your sides and flexible. Too many beginners flap their elbows, bringing their hands out of the proper position and causing their wrists to 'break' or bend when they should remain relatively rigid. The hands are more effective if they are positioned with thumbs up, and keeping your elbows at your side is the best way to ensure that.

4. *Legs*. When used correctly the legs are perhaps the most important aids that a rider has, since they help to control the horse's forward movement. A horse will move away from the pressure of the leg on its sides – forward (or back) if both legs are used, and to the side if pressure is given on only one side.

5. *Heels*, as in 'heels down'. Riders often wonder why it is important to keep heels down if they are not even touching the horse. Note, however, that as you lower your heel, your calf muscles enlarge; this means that without moving your leg, you can apply constant pressure on the horse's side, keeping him moving forward. This is more effective in the long run than constant tapping or kicking with the heel in the horse's side, which can sour a responsive animal. Horses that are insensitive to leg pressure may need a kick with the heels, but this is not a regular practice in good horsemanship – just a quick, effective way of getting a horse to move. A better method is to apply calf pressure first and, if there is no response, to reinforce that pressure with the crop or stick behind your leg. A horse will quickly learn to connect the crop with the application of the leg aid and should begin to respond with only the leg pressure. Many instructors will ask a student to keep their weight in their heels – this is to make sure that the rider's weight does not move too far forward but stays balanced over the centre of the horse's own balance.

6. *Ball of the foot*. This is the strongest part of the human foot and is where the stirrup should be placed. There are several reasons for this: first, the foot will be less likely to slip through the stirrup (or go 'home'), which can be dangerous if the rider is thrown, leaving the foot caught in the stirrup; second, the heel will remain freer to move down if the stirrup is on the ball of the foot rather than the arch; and third, the stirrup won't be as likely to slip off the foot, as it would if it were on the toes.

7. *Seat*. This can refer to the position of the rider in the saddle as in having a good 'seat', or it can refer specifically to the 'seat bones', which are an important aid in riding. There are also, as we have seen, several different kinds of 'seats' or types of equitation. When an instructor speaks of a two-point seat, he means to keep your bottom out of the saddle; a three-point seat means that you should sit down (the three points being the two upper thighs and the rear end). The two-point seat is sometimes called the hunt or half seat.

Movements of the Horse

There are many different movements that a horse can make, some natural, some man-made or artificial, but all requiring a degree of training if the horse is to perform them at the rider's command and with the proper amount of rhythm and control. The names for these different movements and gaits differ considerably from place to place, from breed to breed, and from trainer to trainer so it behoves the horseless rider who travels in a wide circle to learn the names as well as the movements themselves. There is not room here to list all of the variations that exist (these abound in the other horse books I have recommended), but the following tips will, I hope, be of some use to the novice.

1. *Walk*. This is the basic four-beat natural gait at which the rider can establish his or her position in the saddle, either at the beginning of a ride or between the other, faster gaits. The walk can be collected or extended, like the other gaits, meaning that the length of the stride is shortened or increased.

2. *Trot*. There are several types of trot, a two-beat natural gait that is the best gait at which to learn the use of various aids or to school a horse. The slow, collected or sitting trot enables one to sit in relative comfort. The working or rising trot, which is the most common type of trot, requires the rider to rise (move up and down in the saddle) for comfort as well as for

control. The rise is often a difficult technique for the beginner to learn. It should be a simple motion made in rhythm with the horse's movements, which will push the rider naturally out of the saddle. The rider can rise on one of two diagonals, and these are part of the basic vocabulary of equitation. The extended trot, used in dressage, is not simply a speeded-up version but a lengthening of the horse's stride.

3. *Canter*. This three-beat gait is the third natural gait of the horse. The horse canters with one or the other foreleg leading (or on the left or right lead), and the rider can learn to put the horse on the lead he wants by using proper aids. A well-schooled horse can be made to change leads without breaking out of a canter (a flying change); most horses can manage a simple change – dropping back to the trot for a stride or two in order to rebalance for the other lead at the canter. A collected canter looks and feels like a rocking-horse gait; an extended canter is one with a longer stride.

4. *Gallop*. This is a four-beat gait (not just a fast canter), the fastest a horse has. A hand gallop is a controlled gallop where the rider (in a two-point seat) maintains contact with the horse's mouth; a full gallop is all-out with only enough contact to enable the rider to slow the horse when he or she wants. Although a hand gallop is permissible in cross-country riding (indeed necessary in certain equestrian events), a full gallop belongs only on the race course. Many hacking stables put up signs that say 'No galloping' and these should be obeyed. Even race horses are allowed to run full out only occasionally during training when they are not actually in a race.

5. *Pace*. Although some horses have been known to perform this gait naturally, it is an artificial gait invented by humans in which the horse's foreleg and hindleg on each side move forward and back in unison rather than on the diagonal as in a trot. A fast pace is used in harness racing but because it is very uncomfortable for the rider, who is swung from side to side in the saddle, the pace is rarely taught to saddle horses. A very slow pace, or amble, may be found in the occasional riding horse, usually a member of a breed in which the gait is a natural one (a Paso Fino, for example). A variation – called a stepping pace or slow gait – is one of the required gaits in a Five-Gaited saddle horse. The horse appears to be trotting with its forelegs and walking behind, and the resulting gait is comfortable to sit to as well as attractive to watch. Speeded up, the slow gait is known as a rack.

7. *Reinback* or *backing up*. All horses should be trained to move backward, whether they are expected to do so in the school as a pleasure or equitation horse, or out on the trail when movement ahead is impossible. Oddly enough, getting a horse to move back is just like getting it to move forward, except that the reins are held firm to resist the forward motion. Some horses have been trained to move back only with a gentle see-sawing of the reins.

8. *Lateral movements*. A leg yield is accomplished when a horse moves away from the rider's leg pressure, and this may be as simple as bending around a turn or as complicated as moving sideways. Two-tracking, in which a horse moves ahead on the diagonal with forelegs and hindlegs on two different sets of tracks, can be done at the walk, trot and canter. A half pass is a move diagonally toward one side or the other; a side pass is directly sideways. In performing the movements called 'shoulder-in', 'shoulder-out', 'haunches-in' and 'haunches out', the horse moves straight ahead but with the body bent in different ways.

   Turns on the haunches and on the forehand are 180-degree turns in place when the horse holds either his hindquarters or his forelegs still and moves around them to change direction.

3
The Stable

If you have found a stable that provides good instruction, you
may not need to read this chapter all the way through, but for
those of you who already know how to ride or who are looking
around for a new place or a different kind of riding, read on.

There are two basic types of stables to which the horseless
rider can apply — public and private — but within those
categories lie many different variations on the theme. Learning
to understand and play those variations to one's satisfaction
needn't take years — as it did me — so long as you approach the
problem with some forethought and a bit of information about
what to expect and how to analyse what you find. Stables vary
considerably in quality, appearance and cost, but this is one
situation in which a beggar can be a chooser even if he is limited
in time, money and talent. It would cost more, of course, to fly
to France for a week or two of riding at the famous cavalry
school at Saumur, if you were qualified for acceptance, that is,
compared to an investment in a couple of hacks down the road
at the local stable, but those aren't the only alternatives if you
know where and how to look. First, where.

Public Stables

Establishments that specialize in hiring horses to the general
public have been around for thousands of years. Before the
advent of the horseless carriage, the livery stable functioned like
Hertz or Avis, and the hired horse was expected to get its rider
wherever he wanted to go without breaking down along the
way. I suspect that the public stables were run with some
efficiency in those days, treating their animals with a degree of
intelligence so they remained in good working order, although

Anna Sewell's *Black Beauty* reveals that the care was not always humane, particularly on the part of the riders. Often they were not horsemen at all, nor were they even sensitive to the fact that horses, like humans, were capable of feeling pain. Nowadays, of course, public stables do not serve the same function in providing transport, but there are still many of them throughout the country that exist to provide enjoyment to people with an hour or two to spend on the back of a horse. Unfortunately, the pleasure involved in a ride at one of these places is sometimes minimal, even at the best-run stables, which are all too often in the minority.

According to the Riding Establishments Act of 1964, amended in 1970, all stables that hire out horses (or ponies or donkeys) for a charge are required to obtain an annual license from a local authority (either a district or borough council) and to undergo annual inspections to ensure the welfare of the animals and health and safety for both staff and members of the public. The purpose of the Acts was to improve the poor conditions of many hire establishments that had sprung up throughout Great Britain to satisfy an increasing demand for horseback riding. Although more than 2500 stables are now licensed, not all of these maintain the high quality demanded by law, and it is up to the observant rider to determine whether or not a stable meets suitable standards and to approach each unfamiliar stable with a certain amount of caution. The British Horse Society operates what it calls 'an Approvals Scheme', to categorize establishments already licensed; BHS concentrates on facilities that offer instruction, although they also supervise the training standards of horses offered for hire. The BHS approves about 450 of the 2500 licensed establishments and although this number increases annually, there are still many stables that do not carry BHS approval, some because they do not meet the high standards and some because they do not feel the need for BHS approval, although their standards are perfectly adequate.

There are many reasons why a stable may be substandard, not all of them detrimental to either horse or rider. The worst kind of stable is run by someone who is either abusive or uncaring about the animals he hires out; nearly as bad is the ignorant stable owner who does not know what the standards of good and safe care may be.

But a shabby-looking stable may be acceptable in spite of appearances, and in order to analyse a stable's qualifications it is important to know what the stable owner's problems are. For one thing, running a stable – no matter how primitive – costs money, and that investment is very difficult to recoup by simply hiring out horses on an hourly basis. If the weather is bad or if one or more horses is ill or lame, the income goes down but the horses must still be fed and shod; the stable and the tack must still be cleaned and repaired; rates or rent on the property must still be paid. One of the best stables I know – with a full lesson programme, a covered school for bad-weather riding and an enthusiastic group of regular customers – loses money each year. It stays in business because the stable is subsidized by a few wealthy backers, and the manager told me that the only way he could make money would be to deal in buying and selling horses, which the owners would not allow him to do. Stables that are not subsidized must cope with this financial situation in some way, either by scrimping or by offering a less-than-first-class service.

Another major problem faced by stables open to the public is that of safety. No matter how many warnings a rider is given or how many 'ride at your own risk' signs a stable sticks up, there is always the possibility of a lawsuit in case of injury. If a plaintiff can prove that he was given a horse that was unsafe or unsuitable to ride, the stable owner can be liable for damages. One of the regulations of the Riding Establishments Act is that a stable carry sufficient insurance, which is a burdensome, though necessary, expense, but the careful stable owner must also take a cautious attitude. This often means that any rider new to a stable is likely to be given what we tend to call a 'plug', a horse that has to be pushed hard to do more than walk. One stable operator told me that there were only two things a hack had to be: 'four legged and safe'. Such a horse is unlikely to provide much of a ride for anyone, but at least he won't bolt at the first opportunity. Until a stable gets to know an individual rider, that's about all you can expect to be given when you ride. A good stable will require an evaluation test for each new rider and constant supervision unless or until that rider has proved that he can handle a horse at the walk, trot and canter. That kind of individual attention costs the stable money, which is why a good stable will charge more than a poor one, but in this case you are far more likely to get a ride with less likelihood of injury. It may take two or three rides before the manager is convinced to let you have a lively horse, so don't be too impatient and run the risk of ruining your image. Keep in mind that an advanced rider should always be able to get an 'advanced' ride out of any horse, even if it means that you have to push rather than pull. If you've been accustomed to willing, headstrong horses, it's a good experience to get on a slow mover occasionally to remind you what your leg muscles are for.

Many stable managers have told me that their worst problem is the new rider who claims that he has ridden all his life and can handle any horse the stable has. (All horsemen have categories of riders – beginners, intermediates and advanced, but the experienced stable operator has a fourth category – the wise guy.) Although the wise guy's self-evaluation usually recedes somewhat when the horse is brought out for him to mount, all but the most timid will usually try to perpetuate the image – brandishing a crop and trying to gallop off into the distance. Any experienced hack knows how to handle this type even before they get into the saddle, but all too often the episode is an unpleasant one for both horse and rider.

Because inexperienced riders don't usually know enough about riding to handle a horse properly, the average school horse must develop various defence mechanisms to avoid the punishment that their riders invariably deliver. If the horses become too defensive or sour, they become unsuitable for their jobs, and so the turnover in public stables is often rapid, unless the horses are ridden and reschooled by advanced riders once in a while.

We will discuss in more detail the relative merits of the public-stable horse versus the private horse in the next chapter, but the point here is that horses cost money, and good horses cost more than bad ones. Any horse in reasonably good health has some monetary value because of the market for horsemeat, and so even the poorest riding horse will cost a stable a few hundred pounds unless he can be obtained through trade. And a good hack horse, one that will stand up under abuse (inadvertant or not) and still give a good ride or a lesson, is worth his weight in pure gold. In a public stable 'good' has nothing to do with looks or athletic ability and everything to do with temperament and endurance. If you should find a hack that has had the benefit of good breeding and careful schooling you should consider yourself very fortunate indeed.

Stable operators who take care in selecting their horses are wise enough to know that if they can provide good rides to their clients, they will quickly build up a regular business. Some of these stables for the same reason will, in addition to hacking, also offer courses of lessons so that their regular clients will learn enough to enjoy each ride more the next time around. Though there may be no polished brass on the stable door and the tack may be old and well-worn, such an establishment may be just what you are looking for (so long as the place is clean and the tack in good repair). The quality of the lessons will also depend on the experience and personality of the instructor, as we have seen, in addition to the quality of the facilities and the horses themselves. Learning to ride at a public stable is not the only way to go about pursuing an equestrian education, but it is usually the most convenient, and it's worth the extra effort to pick out a good one. Toward the end of this chapter, I will give some suggestions for assessing a stable, but first, some hints about how to find one to assess.

The simplest way to locate a stable is to look in the *Yellow Pages* under 'Riding Schools' (called that even when lessons are not offered) or 'Stables'. The best way is to consult the British Horse Society booklet *Where to Ride*, in which stables are listed according to location and fully described (see page 72),

although this list contains only about 500 establishments and is
therefore rather limited in scope. You can also check the local
newspaper for advertisements or ask at a saddlery shop, which
may know about smaller establishments that don't advertise.
Perhaps the best way is to ask a friend who rides for a
recommendation. Not only can the friend describe for you what
the place is like and how good the horses are, but you will have
the extra advantage of a personal contact. As the old saying
goes, 'It's not *what* you know but *who* you know that counts',
and it's as true in the horse world as anywhere else. As I have
said, stable operators tend to be cautious about sending out a
new rider on one of their better horses, but if a reliable client
recommends you, giving a realistic analysis of your ability,
there's no doubt that you will be given a better horse than the
usual first-timer. Don't risk destroying whatever reputation has
preceded you, however, by acting as if you deserve special
treatment or overestimating your ability. Impatience or
dissatisfaction with a slow horse first time out may lead the
stable management to believe that you haven't got the proper
attitude.

Whether or not you know anyone at the stable, make a
telephone call ahead of time to find out what sort of facilities
they have (school, bridlepaths, indoor ring, etc.), whether they
require an appointment and how much they charge. Costs will
range from £2 to £5 an hour for a hack, depending on the stable
and its location, and lessons will probably be more expensive,
but ask about them anyway. You will probably have to pay
cash in advance for the hack. Ask also whether you will be
allowed to ride by yourself or if you must pay for the services of a
guide and be accompanied by several other riders. Make an
appointment and, when the time comes, get to the stable at
least fifteen minutes ahead so that you can look around. The
extra few minutes will give you a chance to size up the stable
(see page 76) and fall into conversation with other riders or
with members of the stable staff.

Private Stables

A private stable can be as enormous and elegant as an estate where fine race horses are bred and trained, or as simple as the facilities operated by your best friend next door. It may be impossible for you to penetrate the former but the latter is often available to the horseless rider, especially if you are willing to do a bit of work around the stable or exercise the animal when its owner is not around. Riding someone's else's horse under these conditions is usually an attractive opportunity since it is free for the asking (if it's not, you've got yourself into a public stable set-up). But there are a good many things for the horseless rider to keep in mind if the opportunity arises.

First of all, some horse owners may not be receptive to your offer to muck out the box in exchange for a free ride. This isn't selfishness on their part so much as caution, since they could be held liable if you were to fall off or be kicked. Also, they may not feel that you have had sufficient experience to handle the animal properly. Anyone who spends the money to keep a private horse has probably also invested time and energy in schooling it, and allowing an unfamiliar person to ride that horse can result in the animal's acquiring some bad habits or regressing in its education. If you are refused, don't be insulted or assume that they are acting like dogs in their horses' manger. Learn more about riding to convince them that you are capable of handling the animal, and be prepared to sign a release indicating that you will ride at your risk not theirs. On the other hand, if something should happen to the horse while you are riding, you may be held liable for damages, a risk you may not be willing to take. It would be a shame to lose a best friend just for the sake of a free ride, so be sure that you and the horse's owner, best friend or not, are in clear agreement about the responsibilities involved. (See chapter 5 for further information about such legalities.)

While interviewing private owners for this book, I found that some of them were reluctant to hire people on a 'work for a ride' basis, if only because of bad experiences in the past. It takes time and energy to teach someone the proper way to behave around horses and the methods of caring for them, and some people simply don't have that kind of time and energy. Also, because of the risk involved in being around horses – especially highly-strung animals that don't become accustomed to strangers quickly – some owners fear the incidence of injury in their stables to people who are not on their paid staff, or who don't have written permission from parents to ride.

Happily enough, there are a few stable owners sympathetic to the plight of the child (or adult) in need of a horse, since they were in that situation themselves before they had the money to own their own. One of them, a woman with a boarding stable of about fifty horses, told me:

> There is nearly always one horse who needs some loving attention because its owner is away or in college or some such. I do believe that horses need attention over and above the stable care – someone to groom them, chat with them, ride them, etc. Maybe I am sentimental, but I do think that a horse taken care of and loved by a kid looks better. Anyway when I notice a child hanging around a lot, I try to encourage her* and involve her in the stable care. If I get a sense she is really sincere and has the obsession, then I am done for and of course I have to find a horse for her to lease or borrow. I really don't care how well the child rides, for I feel I can always teach that part as well as how to take care of the animal. What really impresses me and persuades me to take on a child is knowing that she is obsessed. As for money, if the child can't afford even half the board, then we usually work out some arrangement – help with the chores, babysitting for my children. I even have one older girl making me a stained-glass window in lieu of several months board. I much prefer this to money, actually.

Needless to say, such understanding and generous souls don't grow on trees, but if you can find yourself a horse owner who has once been horseless, you may be able to win a heart if not a

---

* Her use of the feminine pronoun here indicates the high percentage of female enthusiasts in this activity. The age-old affinity of girls for horses is still true, even past the age of girlhood, but many stable owners and instructors tell me that the percentage of male riders (and adults in general) has increased over the past five years. Men's lib at last?

ride or two. Finding a private stable is not as simple as locating a public stable, since it probably won't advertise unless it offers lessons or livery facilities. Knowing someone who owns a horse or works for such an owner is probably the only way you can get your foot in the stable door. For this reason, veterinarians, farriers and saddlery-shop owners are good people to get to know, although I have myself used any number of other devices (mostly trying to get my friends to buy horses!).

Although I am not particularly aggressive, I do recall one unusual incident that occurred when I was a child. I once found myself wandering down a strange country lane trying to keep busy while my parents were visiting friends nearby. Naturally I found myself drawn like a magnet to a field where a black mare was grazing. She came over to greet me and while we were in conversation, a woman came out of the house next to the field and asked me if I liked to ride. It seems that her daughter had recently sprained an ankle and Inky had been left to languish in the field, unexercised and unloved. Needless to say, I generously offered my services as the lady generously offered me a pair of jodhpurs, and before long I was happily riding along that country lane aboard the deprived Inky.

(Of course, that kind of story is the stuff of which horseless riders' dreams are made, and though it involved pure luck, the moral should be clear: anyone for whom horses are a magnetic force will find a riderless horse sooner or later if one can develop a sixth sense about sprained ankles.)

Schools and Colleges

Some schools and colleges offer riding courses, and a few even have special programmes in horse-related subjects and encourage students to take part in stable management and showing, in addition to providing riding lessons. You will probably have to pay something beyond regular tuition to join the riding programme, but depending on the amount of riding you do, the cost will undoubtedly be less than the cost of keeping your own horse at livery at the school. Schools that specialize in riding will usually advertise their programmes in

horse magazines, as will colleges, but the best way to be sure
about the quality of the facilities and of the course is to
investigate the situation yourself, either in person or by
inquiring of someone who has attended the place.

If you are over school age and looking for an intensive
education in horsemanship without the usual academic set-up
of the college or university, you may be interested in one of the
various institutions that teach only riding and horse-related
subjects. These schools advertise in the horse magazines and
many of them are well worth the cost of tuition. Most of the
people who attend these schools are headed in the professional
direction – as trainers, stable managers, professional riders and
so on, but you needn't have a specific goal in mind when you
apply.

Some of these equestrian centres have residential courses,
with living quarters available for non-residents; others may be
able to suggest nearby lodgings. Several centres specialize in
residential holidays for school children, although many
accommodate adults as well. Check with the BHS *Where to Ride*
booklet for information or write directly to the British Horse
Society (British Equestrian Centre, Kenilworth, Warwickshire
CV8 2LR).

Clubs

Whether you are eight or eighty, there is probably a club that
you can join to pursue your horsy interests with like-minded
companions, even if you don't have a horse of your own. Some
clubs are local, involving very few members and a single stable
facility, while others are national with chapters or local clubs in
various areas throughout the country.

The Riding Clubs Committee of the British Horse Society
administers the group of more than 400 riding clubs in Britain
as well as abroad, with more than 45,000 members (in 1978).
Affiliated clubs must begin with a minimum of 12 members and
activities may include everything from instruction, lectures,
competitions, rides, visits to shows and hunt stables, as well as
social events. Riding Club tests are given to test practical

horsemanship and certificates are awarded each year to entrants who qualify. The idea of the club scheme is to encourage riding as a sport and to improve and maintain the standards of riding, horsemanship, facilities and bridleways.

The year 1979 saw the Golden Jubilee of the Pony Club, whose membership is now over 50,000. Most of Britain's top riders got their start in the Pony Club, which offers equestrian events during school holidays and, in some areas, at weekends. Although much attention is given to teaching the principles of horsemanship to youngsters under the age of 21, most emphasis is on competitive events – gymkhanas (mounted games), horse trials, show jumping, dressage and hunt teams. Qualifying teams may enter national championship events held in each of these activities throughout the year. Most affiliated branches of the Pony Club consist of members who own their own horses or ponies, but horseless or ponyless children are welcome to join, and many gain access to regular mounts loaned by friends or local stables.

Informal clubs not affiliated with the BHS are easy to establish and may take several different forms. Clubs for adults are often a kind of co-operative stable, where horse owners pool their resources to set up facilities to house their animals and keep liability to a minimum. Such clubs can also have advantages for the horseless, who may pay an initiation fee or buy a bond in order to join and then pay a certain amount in dues or expenses for hiring members' horses or taking lessons. If a club does not permit non-owners to join, one can always explore the possibility of co-leasing a horse with a member, sharing the expenses and responsibilities along with the animal.

Equestrian Resorts and Pony Trekking

Although most of these establishments are not designed for regular weekly riding, they can be a wonderful experience for the horseless rider on holiday or over a weekend. Here, too, the facilities and opportunities run from simple one-horse affairs to vast equestrian centres where the instruction is first rate and the horses highly schooled. Room and board are provided together with other holiday activities, such as swimming, and costs will vary according to the programmes and facilities. Some are family-style affairs where meals are served at specific hours with little variation in the menu but a good deal of camaraderie at the table and in the stable, where guests can enter into all phases of farm or stable life. Others are elegant places with formal courses of instruction and special activities, room and laundry service, and restaurant-like dining-rooms. But most are just resorts, where riding is offered as an attraction, like golf, tennis, swimming and the rest.

Before you go to any resort, you should check as you make your reservations just how much time you will be able to spend riding or around the horses and just what the level of instruction (if any) will be. I know of several people who have been disappointed by too little riding or too elementary a programme, though some were able to convince the management to give them special treatment. Riding centres that specialize in instruction and high-level activities such as hunting, eventing and so on will require skill and experience; this can be very satisfying indeed for advanced riders but rather terrifying or at least demoralizing for beginners who arrive unprepared. And trekking centres that cater for people who have never ridden bend over backwards to provide a safe, slow trail ride on quiet animals that would quickly frustrate anyone beyond the beginner level. Be frank and honest over the telephone about your experience and judge the place by their response to your questions. Ask, too, if you will need to take any special clothing or equipment and whether extra charges will be required for any activity.

If you really want to spend your holiday learning, be prepared for work as well as pleasure. A friend of mine had the great privilege of being able to visit Saumur and looked forward eagerly to enjoying the delicious meals and wines along with the fine-blooded horses in the beautiful stables. He relished the idea of hacking through the lovely landscape of field and forest surrounding the château and picking up a few tips from one of the resident cavalry instructors. It turned out, however, that his equestrian ability was found wanting by the instructor to whom he was assigned and he spent his first forty minutes in the saddle practising the sitting trot. By the time he finally got back to the château, he was far too tired and sore to drink in all the beauties to say nothing of the wine.

If you simply want to relax, however, by taking comfortable and undemanding trail rides through the countryside, there are plenty of fine places that offer that – both here and abroad. In addition to the BHS booklet check travel brochures, horse magazine advertisements and other sources of information about resorts, trekking holidays, pack trips and other types of equestrian holidays. Most of the National Parks have public riding stables nearby or on the premises, and there are many organizations throughout the world that specialize in holidays on horseback, some involving overnight trips or week-long treks led by experienced guides.

Most treks originate from a centre, either residential or non-residential, from which daily rides are taken along various routes, returning to base camp in the evening. Post trekking is the term used for rides that camp out overnight or stop at inns or hotels along the route, often up to five days in extent. Obviously, trekking is restricted to areas with suitable countryside for long rides and the ponies used in these areas tend to be local breeds. Dartmoor, Exmoor, the New Forest, Cumbria, Yorkshire and Northumberland are the most popular areas for trekking in England; Wales and, in Scotland, Tayside, Highland, Strathclyde and Grampian would seem to be the most likely regions.

Experienced riders should be warned that trekking involves mostly riding at the walk, with occasional trots, since the rides are geared to beginners, but even those who do not ride would be advised to learn a little horsemanship in advance in order to enjoy the trip more thoroughly. Certainly the novice should inform the trekking centre in advance that a quiet, safe animal is required. Some substandard trekking centres catering for beginners use underfed animals to ensure a quiet ride, but these

animals can also be unsafe, and so I recommend that you select
only those centres approved by one of the following societies:
The British Horse Society, the National Pony Society, the
Ponies of Britain, the Pony Trekking Society of Wales or the
Scottish Trekking and Riding Association. The Ponies of
Britain publishes a list describing many of the approved
trekking and riding holiday centres.

Stable Analysis

Though it hardly seems worth the effort to analyse a stable if all
you're investing in is an hour's ride, a quick look around the
place to size it up can make the difference between an enjoyable
ride and an indifferent or poor one. Even if a stable is the only
one in town, your decision about *how* to approach it rather than
whether to approach it at all can influence your rides there,
since the first is not likely to be the last if it is a good one. Even if
the ride or the horse or the stable is lacking in some important
way, you might be able to do something to improve the
situation your next time out.

Handsome is as handsome does, and the attractiveness of a
stable is only important if it is supported by an efficient
management. Beautiful rolling pastures and spanking clean
stalls with polished brass labels are lovely to look at but not
altogether necessary. I know of several good stables where the
paddocks are relatively small, and the stables are in need of
paint, and yet the horses are turned out regularly and the boxes

are cleaned thoroughly each morning. What a stable may lack in terms of money for property and superficial improvements it may spend wisely on knowledgeable help, good management and decent horses. When you tour your prospective stable, look for the following:

1. A well-lit stable with sizeable loose boxes that are sturdily built and safe, with no visible hazards, such as broken glass, protruding nails or boards, and pitchforks lying about.

2. A staff of grooms or stable people – at least one to every five horses – who are working at something as you pass by, whether it be mucking out, grooming, feeding, cleaning tack or something horse-related.

3. An array of tack in good repair. The saddles don't have to be expensive but they should be well made and well fitting (to the horse if not to the rider). Before you mount look under the saddle flaps to make sure that the girth is whole and that the billets are securely fastened to the saddle. Check the stirrup leathers as well. Signs of repair aren't necessarily bad but the repairs should have been done well, not with string or baling wire. Check the bridle, too, to make sure that there aren't pieces of leather about to break, especially on the reins.

4. A collection of horses standing in stalls or loose boxes with relatively fresh bedding underfoot, good ventilation and buckets of water available. If the animals are in stalls, they should be tied by a lead rope attached to the halter, not by the reins. If they are tacked up, the girths should be loose. If you notice that your eyes are watering from the stench, you will probably notice that the horses are suffering, too. Point this out to the stable manager and if he or she reacts angrily, don't ride there but report the situation to the local branch of the RSPCA.

5. Notice whether the horses themselves appear to be in good condition – groomed and generally healthy looking. Saddle sores, a sign of ill-fitting tack, should not be in evidence, but

if they are they should be obviously medicated or somehow protected if the horse is to be ridden. Overgrown hooves, loose or missing shoes, untreated open sores or cuts and general filth are signs of neglect and poor management. Don't leap to conclusions if you see some ribs showing or a few small scars here and there, but if the horses are in obvious distress because of poor treatment, report the situation to the authorities.

6. The stable manager or an assistant should be present to supervise the hiring procedure and be available for any questions, which ought to be answered with some degree of care. The manager of a stable is a busy person and does not always have the time to spend on what he considers minor details, but you should be able to get some satisfaction from the person in charge — especially where it concerns your own ride. If no one on the staff takes the time to see that you are properly mounted on a horse you can handle, beware.

7. Are there signs posted in the stable about safety? No smoking signs are critically important, as are warnings about riding too fast or recklessly, bringing a 'hot' (overworked and sweating) horse back to the barn, regulations about footwear and headgear, and so on.

8. Look around at the people who are riding at the stable. Are they properly dressed? Ask one or two people who look like regulars how long they have ridden at this stable and how they like it. You can also ask about the horses and which are the favourites. Remember always that one person's favourite may be another person's runaway, but it's always good to know — if you have the choice — which are the problem animals and which ones will give a pleasant, safe ride.

9. One sign of a good stable is the questioning process the management gives the prospective rider. Are you asked to sign a release? Do they write down your address (in case of accident)? Your experience? If so, the management is probably right-minded. Even better is an insistence on an evaluation test.

10. Does the manager insist on a guide for hacking out? If you are new to the stable, you will not know the bridle paths, so this is a sensible rule from your point of view, but it is also a necessary safety precaution on the part of the stable owner who has never seen you ride before.
11. Do the people on the stable's staff seem to know how to handle the horses they are caring for? Don't confuse firm handling with abuse if you see someone swat a horse's rump to get him to move, but be alert to abuses such as yanking on reins to lead a horse, hitting a horse unnecessarily or letting one stand in the sun for an extended period of time without any water and laden with tack as it awaits the next rider.

These questions are the essential eleven, but there may be others that will come to your mind as you look around the stable. If you have made a reservation for a ride at a certain hour, be sure to arrive early to give yourself a chance to take this all-important tour. If you are not pleased by what you see, you can always cancel the appointment. If you are not allowed to walk around the stable, find out why. If it's a question of convenience to the staff who are busy getting the horses ready, ask if you may look around on your own, assuring them that you will not get in the way. If that request, reasonably tendered, is refused, you may have to limit your analysis to what you can see as you wait for your horse. On one occasion – at a truly awful city stable where we suspected ill management – my husband and I were rudely refused permission to see the boxes where the hack horses were kept. Happily, the drinks machine was near the stable door and we could sneak a look while innocently finishing our drinks near the machine. A stable hand did try to shoo us away from the door but we managed to get a good look at what were, of course, intolerable conditions for horse or human. In this case, the real tip-off was the attitude of the stable manager.

If you are visiting a private stable – especially if it's just a stable with one or two horses in it – you will undoubtedly have a

An ideal riding establishment, with a roomy stable, a sizeable outdoor ring for lessons, a covered school (above right) for bad weather and an office (top left)

better chance to look around, but the investigation will be very different, if indeed you can make one at all in any obvious sense, especially if the ride is going to be a free one on a friend's horse. Pointing out broken tack or a messy stall would most definitely not be a polite response to the offer of a free ride, but you can couch those observations in an offer to muck out a stall or get the rein repaired yourself. That way the owner will be aware of the problem and might even thank you for pointing it out. Even if you end up with the responsibility of following through, you'll at least have the satisfaction of knowing that a wrong has been righted and that you'll always be welcome in this particular stable.

The old saying 'Don't look a gift horse in the mouth' (which was of course referring to the animal's age and the fact that a free horse, regardless of age, was a bargain) does apply to some extent in accepting a free ride. If the stable where the gift horse is kept looks pretty shabby and the horse looks out of·condition and poorly cared for, you would probably not enjoy yourself much, no matter how insistent your friend might be about getting you to ride. But casual appearances can be deceiving. I remember going once to a stable on the recommendation of the owner of a small hotel in an unfamiliar town, and being allowed to make myself at home without any supervision. The owner's son, who was busily mowing the lawn, said 'Sure, you can ride. Just take a bucket of oats up to that pasture there and catch the first horse who comes to you. The saddles and stuff are in the barn.'

Luckily for both me and the horse, I knew enough at that point to ask the boy what the horses' names were so that I could match the right saddle and bridle to the right horse. And I knew enough to groom the horse, pick out its hooves and put the tack in the proper places before heading off into the woods for what turned into a delightful afternoon. Most owners aren't quite so cavalier about their animals, but if they are, you are obliged to be even more responsible about using the animals than you would be riding under the owner's nose.

On another occasion, a woman whose daughter was away at

school was delighted to let me exercise the horse that had been virtually abandoned. Before I could ride, I had to repair the neglected bridle and during the ride, I noticed that the horse was breathing very heavily even after a slow trot. My husband, a veterinarian, watched the animal move and, taking the horse's lack of conditioning into account, was able to diagnose a case of emphysema. Luckily for the horse this time, we managed to convince the woman to put the horse on medication and to change its diet of hay to a dustfree pelleted feed that would not aggravate his already stressed lungs.

After you have looked over the prospective stable and made your analysis of the management, the general condition of the building, the horses and the equipment, you should look a little beyond the stable itself to see what kind of facilities there are for riding. Is there an enclosed area in which you can school a horse, warm it up before a ride or get the kinks out as the case may be? Is the area large enough for several people to use at once without getting on each other's nerves – or tails? If there is a course of lessons, will individual riders not taking lessons be able to use the ring? Is there an indoor school that can be used in the winter, at night and on rainy days? Is it lighted or heated? (One indoor school I know was constructed like a plastic bubble and although it was light, it also was extremely cold on winter days – at least ten degrees below the outside temperature.) If there is no school at all, is there an area near the stable that can be used as an improvised ring – a level, relatively large piece of ground with good solid footing?

If the stable specializes in hacking, are there several paths or only one? Are those paths relatively open or are they narrow and overhung with trees? Have deep holes, rocky areas and other potential dangers been spotted and marked? Are there parts of the path that come close to or cross metalled roads? Have large branches been trimmed so that they don't interfere with the horses and riders? One city stable I know hires horses for riding in a park, which has some very nice old trails where riders must share the space with joggers, prams and children on bikes, to say nothing of people who enjoy frightening horses by throwing rocks or jumping into the path unexpectedly. These urban hazards may not bother the experienced urban horse, but the rider should be prepared for sudden fits and starts. Riding in company may be better in these cases than riding alone.

If there are several bridle paths and the stable does not offer a guide, is there a map you can use to make sure you don't get lost and that you get your horse back on time? Are there jumps set up along the way and will you have permission to take them? If you don't want to jump, are there paths around the jumps so that you'll have a choice?

Private stables may well have training schools, fields with hunt courses set up or lovely paths around the property, but in suburban areas, a horse kept in a garden may involve riding across property belonging to other people. Before you set off on your borrowed horse, make sure that you find out where you will be allowed to ride and which areas are out of bounds. People who do not own horses may not appreciate hoofprints in their gardens or across their newly seeded fields, and you may do yourself and other horsemen a disservice by disobeying the rules of polite conduct by riding there without permission. (See chapter 5 for the etiquette of bridle path riding.)

4
The Horse

The rider who approaches a stable for a ride, whether or not a fee is involved, may not have any chance to select the animal that is going to be his or hers. Public stables worth patronizing will probably select the horse for you based on your experience (or on what you tell them and what they can tell of you), and a free ride on a private horse is probably offered for that animal alone. Although an instructor may allow a pupil to pick a favourite mount, most teachers will assign horses according to what they are attempting to teach. Nevertheless, there is some element of choice involved on the rider's part, even if it's to change horses in midstream or not to ride at all. In other words, analysing the stable is not the whole story in deciding whether or not you want to ride (or be taken for a ride, as the case may be). The horse needs some analysing, too, before you put your feet into the stirrups. What follows is a special on-the-ground approach.

Selecting a Horse

Most horse books start off with a chapter called 'Selecting a Horse' covering the fine points of breed, conformation, colour and so on. None of these aspects of horse selection, practically speaking, will matter to the horseless rider, but there are a few points worth noting. Whether you are offered one of those members in low standing of the equine set – the hack or school horse – or a carefully tended private horse, which can be anything from a sour pony to a full brother of Red Rum, keep your eyes and your mouth open. In other words, look carefully at the horse and ask a lot of questions.

The rider's choice: a sleepy 'plug', an under-exercised, over-excited nag and a calm, well-mannered animal

Breed

Generally speaking, the average public-stable horse is a mixed-breed horse, the equine equivalent of a mongrel, where experience and past history are more important than pedigree. A private horse, on the other hand, is likely to be a better sort of animal, perhaps a purebred with papers, perhaps not, but undoubtedly the object of better care, which can make him a superb performer, a spoiled brat or something in-between. Exceptions to this general rule abound, of course, for I have found many public stables with one or two fine purebreds in the wings for advanced riders, and I have known any number of private mongrels. But the public purebreds are usually long in the tooth, with their best years behind them, while the private grades can range from cheeky youngsters to wise old Dobbins. Nevertheless, if you are offered a purebred to ride, you should approach it rather differently from the way you would approach a grade or a crossbred. Finely bred animals will have certain characteristics of their breed and may require relatively delicate handling on the part of the rider.

A thoroughbred may (or may not) have been bred for the track, and he is likely to be high-spirited and fast, given his head (which is not a good idea). Arabs are trained in many different ways – as dressage horses, as hunters and as contributors to most other light-horse breeds – and any purebred Arab is likely to be a handful. More recently popular breeds, such as the Trakhener and Hanoverian, have become fine dressage horses. Ponies come in all shapes and sizes, of course, so long as the size doesn't go over fourteen-and-a-half hands (fifty-eight inches from ground to withers) and each one of them has a different attitude toward life and people, and a different set of talents and temperament.

Crossbreds, where the breeding has been planned for particular reasons, may be treated like purebreds in that they will have certain identifiable, built-in traits. The Irish hunter, for example, is a cross between a thoroughbred – full of speed and athletic ability – and a heavier almost draft-horse type – full of the strength so necessary to carry big riders over treacherous ditches and uneven terrain. Anglo-Arabs are thoroughbred-Arab crosses, very satisfactory animals for many purposes.

'Grade' or mixed-breed horses may show some breed traits and for the most part, they are the mongrels of the horse world – and while that may mean 'low-class' in the social department, it also means unique and adaptable in practical terms, to be judged on the basis of experience and personality rather than looks or innate characteristics.

Sex

Unless you are at a breeding farm or stud, sex isn't a subject that usually rears its interesting head around a riding stable. Most school horses are geldings (castrated males) which tend to be steadier in temperament than mares or stallions, who often have each other on their minds rather than the business of obeying human commands. I once had my ankle broken by a mare who was in heat and simply furious at the gelding I was riding, so frustrated that she kicked out at him and got me instead. Many experts feel that mares are more sensitive than geldings and make wonderful competition horses for that reason, but even they will admit that a mare in heat just before an important event can be a disadvantage to the rider. I have ridden many mares as school horses and in private stables, and I would agree that they are more alert and perhaps even smarter than the average mixed-breed gelding, but if you want to be sure of a relatively safe ride, a gelding is your best bet. They aren't all angels, of course, since a bad experience can make a rogue out of any horse, regardless of sex, but they are far less complicated than stallions, who should probably not be handled except by expert riders who know them well.

Conformation

According to one stable manager I talked with, the only points of conformation or horse anatomy worth noting by the horseless rider are that a horse have four sound legs. And it's true that the rider setting out for a short ride needn't concern him- or herself with the horse's appearance unless there are a lot of obvious faults. Roman noses are traditionally worn by stubborn horses, and high-withered equines won't be very comfortable to ride bareback, but beyond this, the average horse needn't be looked at too closely if you're not planning to invest in his future after your hour is up. Very short or tall people may want to ride relatively short or tall horses, and heavy-set men should obviously aim toward heavy-set horses capable of carrying them out of sight of the stable. But most riders of average size should be able to deal with average-sized equines, whether they are fifteen hands or seventeen. On the other hand, signs of illness or previous injury that may result in a bad ride should be observed and noted, even by the occasional rider. Saddle sores should be treated and protective padding used under the saddle; a horse that breathes heavily after only a little exertion should not be worked very hard if at all; a horse with a very shabby coat, oversized belly and listless disposition may be infested with internal parasites (worms) and may not be strong enough to manage anything more than a gentle walk-trot session. Any symptom of lameness should be checked immediately, and if no obvious cause is present (such as a loose shoe or a stone imbedded in the hoof or frog) and if the lameness doesn't work itself out within three or four minutes of walking, the horse should be led, not ridden, back to the barn. (I admit to knowing one hack who was clever enough to invent a lame foreleg every time he felt a saddle touching his back; the threat of being sent back to the dealer's managed somehow to cure him, though we still can't figure out how he knew.)

You don't have to read a veterinary manual or insist on a veterinarian's presence before you ride, but you should make a point of watching normal horses at work so that anything unusual in a horse's appearance or gait is obvious to you at a glance. If you do notice something amiss – or if the animal is wearing what seems to you an unusual assortment of boots and bandages on his legs – ask the owner or manager about his condition and follow their instructions about using him (or not). Some busy stable managers may miss slight problems and they will (or should) be grateful to you for noticing or taking the trouble to care. If the management doesn't seem to care as much as you do and brushes you off with an unsatisfactory explanation, you should – if you are certain that the horse is suffering pain – report the case to the local branch of the RSPCA. But don't jump to conclusions unless you are sure; be persistent enough to check the situation with the groom that tends the horse and to have an expert horseman confirm your findings.

Colour

People in the market for a horse often have preferences about a horse's colour ('I just have to get a chestnut, Mother, because it will go so nicely with my new jodhpurs,' and stuff like that). Except for a few genetic experts who have determined that some colours are dominant traits in certain breeds, and allowing that some public-stable operators tend to avoid gray horses (because the dirt shows more readily), almost everyone would agree that colour is only skin deep. For the purposes of a rider looking for a comfortable, pleasant ride, the only colour that matters to the horseless rider is green. An inexperienced (green) horse will probably know less about the fine art of equitation than you will, and if you are a beginner, you should avoid that animal. Most experts agree that the best horse on which to learn the basics is one that knows more than the rider, and a well-mannered, well-schooled horse is a treasure to any instructor. Some friends of mine, green as grass but enthusiastic as they come, bought a seven-year-old Arab gelding right out of the show ring and soon realized that they had to take a few lessons to catch up with the horse. Once they learned about collection, extension and leg yields, their appreciation for the horse grew with every ride. (The nice part of this story, actually, is that they were able to teach King about hacking, for he was accustomed to travel only on well-combed paths, preferably in the shape of a showring. He ignorantly ploughed through the brush, stumbling over rocks and being frightened by rabbits until my friends gave him sufficient exposure to the horrors of the wilderness. At last report, he was still teaching and being taught.)

If you are about to take a lesson or be led out on the bridle path by a guide, you needn't worry too much about getting into trouble, since you will be under supervision, and, if you are at a good place, you will have been given a horse whose manners and habits are well known to the person in charge. If you are going out on your own, however, you should try to find out as much about the horse's past history as possible before getting into the saddle.

Some useful questions to ask are:
1. Does the horse go best with light contact on the reins, strong hands, or a loose rein? (Remember that some horses speed up with a tight rein and slow down with a loose rein.)
2. Does the horse have any bad habits, such as kicking, shying, bolting, wheeling, rolling into puddles and ponds and so on? If so, you'll have to keep clear of other horses, avoid or be prepared for scary spots, keep a good firm hand and leg on the animal, and otherwise stay alert to trouble.
3. Does the horse have any special phobias? Some horses are afraid of dogs, of certain spots along the path, of crossing bridges or going under them, of walking through water or of horses that come too close behind or get ahead of them. Some even have special aversions to one or two stablemates. I once spent a delightful summer schooling a pony at a zoo and found, to my surprise, that he shied away from one particular corner in the camel-riding ring that we used. It turns out that this pony had a real terror of elephants (not camels) and that this corner was next to the elephant house. We soon taught him to treat that corner like any other, but riding in parades was never a real pleasure unless we could get a camel between us and the elephants to give zoogoers the impression that domesticated animals were easier to handle than wild ones!
4. Does the horse have the habit of eating grass or leafy

branches along the trail? This isn't a particularly serious fault, although I've known several people who have been pulled right out of the saddle because of piggy horse behaviour. It's always best to be prepared to keep a firm rein if you are going through succulent-looking farm country.

5. In jumping, does the horse tend to run out, stop or jump willingly? Even if you know that a horse has been jumped, don't try it on the trail the first time out unless you are in company with an experienced rider. I remember once trying to leap a log on an old mixed-breed gelding only to find that the experience triggered in him some old memory about chasing something or other and off we went. Another time I tried to get a healthy, otherwise willing pony over a small fence between pastures only to find that he had been trained never to cross such a barrier. After one spill, a lot of soothing encouragement on my part and a number of stronger words, I gave up and we went off in search of an open pathway.

6. Is the horse a 'stable rat' – reluctant to leave the stable alone and determined to race back to it the moment he is turned in the direction of home? Such a horse needs reschooling to break the habit, but for the occasional rider, one needs a firm sense of determination (and perhaps another horse and rider) on the way out and a firm grip on the reins on the way in. I've known horses who could put on a tremendous act of exhaustion until they were headed homeward, at which point they would suddenly develop a whole new interest in life and a new spring to their step. (This, incidentally, is not altogether a bad fault if you are riding an unfamiliar path; the chances are that the horse will be able to find his way home even though you are convinced that the two of you are completely lost.)

If the answers to all of these questions lead you to believe that you're about to board the worst-mannered, least agreeable animal in the world, or even if they make you a bit apprehensive, don't fret. And try not to let your apprehension show, because you will risk transmitting some nervousness to the horse, making disobedience likely. If you know that a horse has a habit or two that may show up during a ride, you will always be in a better position (literally) to prevent it if you are prepared, or to deal with it if you get into an unavoidable situation. Sometimes such questions cannot be answered, either because there is no one around to do so or because there isn't time. One friend of mine, while visiting a farm in Ireland, had the good fortune to be there when the pack of hounds, which was being shown off to him, caught a scent and began racing off to follow it. The owner and his staff quickly saddled up a few of the horses for their visitors and our friend was led up to a mare he had never seen before. 'Anything I should know?' he nervously asked the groom who was giving him a leg up. 'She'll take care of you,' came the reply and off they went. It soon became apparent that the mare knew much more about the whole business than our friend – and she carried him safely for an hour's gallop (or so it seemed) over terrain that she knew as well as her own paddock, over ditches and hedges that were four times as imposing as the crossrails he was used to at home. But all he had to do was stick to the saddle, keep his balance, grab a handful of mane and let her do her thing with as little interference as possible. After the experience, he breathlessly admitted that he had never before felt more exhilarated and more terrified at the same time.

With the average hired horse, naturally, you can't always consider yourself on such a capable, willing animal. But don't under-estimate the ability of any horse, especially a hack horse. Some people maintain that horses aren't as intelligent as pigs, but hired horses are as smart as you are – and with good reason. All those jabs in the mouth – inadvertent or not – from riders of every shape and ability (or lack of it) haven't gone unnoticed, and such a horse invariably picks up a whole array of tricks to avoid getting hurt. Throwing the head up or lowering it to evade the bit, grabbing the bit in the teeth to get control of the situation, and keeping a stiff neck or a rubbery one to avoid bit pressure are only a few. Some horses when they anticipate abusive treatment will bolt off at the first chance, bucking as they go to put the rider off balance, and others will just not go at all – or at least not at any perceptible speed. A few horses I've met will do just as they please, disobeying commands as rapidly as they are given. It isn't only a mule that is stubborn, and it isn't only an elephant that remembers. A hired horse who doesn't want to do something can be pretty determined not to do it, and once he gets away with something (which is usually the case with novice riders), he'll remember that for a long time and get away with it until an expert gets hold of him.

But the approach to take with these animals is not anger or rough handling. Respect the horse and try to figure out why he is that way. Disobeyed commands may be the result of many confused hours suffering at the hands and legs of riders who pull and push at the same time. Bolting off into the blue may have become a habit of the horse who has had more than one 200-pound rider plunk himself unceremoniously into the saddle. Such horses deserve reschooling as well as respect, but if you are only aboard for an hour, you can count on getting a pretty good lesson, even if there isn't a human instructor in sight.

I remember one particular animal, a rather fine mare who had a considerable knowledge of dressage movements and a pronounced dislike of people who sat too far forward. She had had a sore on her withers a few years before I rode her and never forgot the pain, even though the injury had healed along ago. My instructor had not been able to convince me in words that leaning forward was a bad habit of mine, but one short hour on this mare cured me forever. Every time my centre of balance got ahead of hers, she would stop short and back up until I got into the proper position. Believe me, one hour of backing around a ring when all the other riders were going forward was an embarrassing though effective forward step in my education!

Another horse I remember had a real hatred of heels in his side, especially on the near (left) side, I suppose as a result of a spur-dragging rider in his past. My instructor used this horse to teach her pupils to rely on calf pressure rather than heels and to keep their lower legs from flopping around in the stirrups. That lesson I spent going sideways in a series of side passes that would have done a Lippizaner proud, except that I had never given a deliberate cue for that particular dressage movement and quickly learned to be aware of the position of my feet.

Some school horses aren't nearly as predictable, however, and that's because they are subjected to many different riders. One horse whose name (Sneakers) will remain permanently engraved on my mind (and knee) was an honest if not talented jumper whom I used to ride regularly in weekly lessons. One session, however, he started running out to the right at every fence and eventually sent me careening in a rather spectacular fall that wrenched my knee. Obviously someone had 'taught' him in a previous hour how to drop his right shoulder and wheel to the side by letting him get away with the trick once and then again, so that by the third time the running out had become a pattern. The horse was successfully reschooled by my patient instructor and a more severe bit, but *I* learned a lesson, too, which was never to take a school horse for granted.

Private horses also have their special habits – and though they may not be sour from years of poor or ignorant riders, they are perhaps even more of a challenge for the first-time rider, especially if they have become accustomed to one particular person in the saddle. It seems as though they act like school children with a substitute teacher and try to make as much trouble as possible just to see what they can get away with. It is more likely, however, that the unfamiliar rider has aroused their suspicions just because he or she is unfamiliar. Obviously one must ask the owner or regular rider for any tips, but even so the horse should be approached with special care and no rough handling, if only because giving a private horse bad habits or a bad experience will soon make you a *persona non grata* around that stable. Sometimes the owner may not even be aware that there is a problem. A horse owned by a friend of mine always – without fail – broke into a canter at one point on the bridle path near her house, and simply wouldn't stay at a walk, no matter what I did. It turned out that this spot was the first safe place to canter and that my friend invariably asked for a canter at that point. It wasn't until she saw me having such trouble with her suddenly headstrong horse that she realized how well the horse had trained *her*. (Reschooling the horse, incidentally, was not too difficult: we simply took a different route away from the stable and after a half hour of good exercise tried the usual path. By this time the horse was agreeable to walking past the critical spot. A few days of this, first walking and then trotting, was sufficient to keep the horse under control and responsive to deliberate cues rather than geographical landmarks.)

Generally speaking, private horses tend to be more athletic and willing than hired ones, needing less of a strong hand and more of a delicate contact with the mouth, less of a strong leg and more of a secure, balanced seat. If a horse has been trained to specific aids, you should know this before you start out (or you may not be able to stop); if a horse should be ridden on a loose rein rather than with constant bit contact, unless you know this you may find yourself on an animal that will resist every cue you give, running ahead when you think you are asking for a slower gait or a halt. The under-exercised private horse can also be full of high spirits that feel a lot like bad manners if those spirits involve bucking or heading off for the hills. Horses that haven't had regular exercise, however, shouldn't be worked hard until they are conditioned sufficiently to handle it. Make your first few rides short and easy, gradually building up the length of the ride and the amount of exertion until the horse is fit.

Approaching the Horse

All of this talk about breed, sex, conformation and experience is only part of your analysis of the animal you are about to mount. Obviously, if you are presented with a feisty little Arab stallion, complete with lame foreleg and a decidedly green colour, you would be advised to say 'No, thanks'. And if someone leads out an experienced, well-seasoned gelding who knows his way around, you should probably feel privileged at the chance to ride him. Your choices won't, of course, be quite so dramatic, but you should be able to get some impression of a horse's way of going long before you mount up by taking a good, hard look at him before you make a commitment and by asking some of those penetrating questions if you have a chance to do so.

If the horse presented to you looks like a handful that you're not prepared to handle or confident enough about, you are perfectly within your rights to refuse. Busy stable managers with only a limited number of horses at their disposal may object or refuse your request for a substitution, claiming that they don't have any other animal to offer. This may be true, and you may not be able to ride, but if you feel insecure enough to make the request, you'll be better off not riding at all than risking a bad experience. Most stable managers – like *Maîtres d'hôtel* at busy restaurants – can usually come up with a suitable alternative, however, and it is their obligation by law to provide just that. Although stable signs may insist that the hirer agrees to ride at his or her own risk, the management is liable if it puts anyone who requests a 'quiet, safe horse' on one that is neither quiet nor safe. (See the section on legal considerations in chapter 5.) Since public stables tend to cater for people who have never set foot in stirrup, their stables are (or should be) full of horses that are accustomed to novices, and the chances are that you will be able to find yourself a suitable mount.

Now you have reached the moment you've been waiting for. You have studied the stable and found it and its instructor acceptable; you have studied the horse and found him rideable. But before you get into the saddle, take another moment or two on the ground and forget the generalities you've just read. Look the horse in the eye and let him know right from the start that you are fully prepared for whatever lies in store. At this point, self-confidence (even if you feel none) is more important than the fit of your boots. For during the time that you've been analysing him, the horse has undoubtedly been sizing you up himself. It is impossible to put oneself into a horse's polo-ball-sized brain, but his internal analysis may be going something like this:

'This rider is going to be a real winner. She's a bit afraid of me I can tell, because she's nervous about getting into the saddle. She's not really sure how to hold the reins and, wouldn't you know, she going to stick me in the side with her left foot and thump down on my back when she mounts! I wonder if she knows about Weight Watchers . . . This is going to be fun – I think I'll wait until we get around that bunch of trees up ahead and then I'll show her what it feels like to land hard – right on the ground!'

Or, perhaps in your case, it will go like this: 'That's nice, this guy really knows what he's doing. He doesn't seem to worry about whether I'm going to step on him and his reassuring pat on the neck is definitely a good sign. He seems pretty thoughtful about seeing that the girth isn't pinching me on the belly and he can adjust the stirrups without asking for help. I might give him a buck or two just to be sure, but this is going to be a pleasure, I'm sure.'

If all of this seems far-fetched – we all know horses aren't very smart – think again. Horses are sensitive creatures, having spent many hundreds of years in human company, and they are probably more expert at sizing up potential riders than we are at figuring them out. Don't let this equine superiority get the better of you, however. You are, after all, a member of a presumably more intelligent species and even if the horse may be stronger and wiser in his ways than you are, you can be master of the situation if you use your head and approach the animal with a positive, confident manner. It will be worth convincing him that you are on the side of the angels – not a potential devil on horseback.

Some time ago, I read a curious book by Henry Blakely called *Talking with Horses* (Souvenir Press). The author is well known for taming difficult horses and for communicating with the animals he rides, and over the years he has devised a method by which people can understand what it is that horses 'say' and what it is that they like to hear. Of course he is referring to gesture as much as to actual sound or language, but his discussion of horse talk is very interesting indeed, mainly because he has a real insight into the way the species naturally behaves. Some of his observations are useful for humans

meeting a horse for the first time, since they are based on what
horses do when meeting each other. When you approach an
unfamiliar horse, for instance, breathe gently into his nostrils
and let him breathe into yours. Silly as it sounds, that tends to
have a soothing effect, rather like a human handshake,
indicating that you mean no harm and can be trusted. Another
reassuring thing to do is to lay your arm across the top of a
horse's neck, somewhere between the ears and the withers. If
you watch friendly horses in a pasture, you will notice that one
will occasionally lay his neck across the neck of the other. This
trick isn't guaranteed to work on a rogue who is dead set on
kicking you into the next county, but it's worth trying on any
animal you suspect of distrust or uneasiness in your presence.
(Also, you are standing in a place where a kick is difficult, if
that's what is on his mind.)

   Even rank novices around horses know that flattened ears
mean trouble and that a cocked hind foot should be given as
much room as possible to avoid a kick. But there are many other
signs of equine disturbance that an eager horseman should
learn to interpret. A horse that paws at the ground while
standing is impatient to be doing something else. If he 'nods for
rein' and keeps wanting you to loosen up, he's probably bored
and needs to be taken in hand and encouraged to work harder.
If he shows you the white of his eye, he is nervous or frightened
by something or other, and if he swishes his tail while you are
riding – even though the fly season is long gone – he's disturbed
by something that you are doing, such as giving an inaccurate
or confusing cue, using a rein that is too tight or simply making
him do something he doesn't like to do. You'll pick up these
signals and more just by being around horses, but even at the
start, it's important that you take a 'learning' approach toward
every horse you meet. Even more important, however, is that
you let the horse know that you are confident for, like dogs,
horses can quickly sense fear or insecurity in humans. If you let
yours show, the horse is likely to take advantage in some way.
Don't allow self-confidence to be displayed as bravado, because
a horse can also sense the insecurity that lies behind it. Just be

quiet, self-assured and deliberate in your movements, handling
the horse with as little fuss and hesitation as possible. A
hyperactive or dangerous-looking horse will need a different
approach, but if you don't know how to deal with that, ask for
another horse.

The First Ride
Now that we have selected the horse and analysed him, let's get
aboard. Chances are that the first few minutes in the saddle will
be a continuation of the testing process that was begun on the
ground, so keep alert to the situation. You may have to undergo
a couple of unpleasantries, such as the horse's moving on while
you are mounting, refusing to go forward once you are in the
saddle, resisting your commands or even delivering a buck or
two – not enough to unseat you but enough to upset your
balance and unsettle your peace of mind. As soon as the horse
figures out that you know how to handle these tricks of the
trade, he'll probably give up and let you take charge. But
instead of going through this initiation, you will gain the
animal's respect a lot more quickly if you take charge from the
start – and that includes the attitude that you are the tester, not
the testee. You'll save valuable time (which for an hour's ride
may be worth as much as a pound) by preparing yourself right
from the time you leave the ground. Here are some tips.

1. First, make sure the girth is tight.
2. If the horse moves away from you while you are mounting,
   hold the reins properly to prevent this by keeping pressure
   on the off (right) side of the horse. If this doesn't work after
   a couple of tries, ask someone to hold the horse for you or to
   give you a leg up. If you only have an hour to ride, don't
   waste time schooling a horse you may never see again and
   don't feel embarrassed about needing assistance. If no one
   is there to help you, use a mounting block if there is one or
   any convenient object to get you into the general vicinity of
   the left stirrup.

3. While you are mounting, don't stick the horse in the side with your left toe, which will only give him an excuse to move ahead before you are ready. And when you sit, do so as lightly as possible. Most horses resent having a hundred pounds or more flopping unceremoniously down on their backs or banging their kidneys.

4. When you get your stirrups adjusted to the correct length (and ask for help if you need it), doublecheck the girth. And then get yourself – your position in the saddle, your legs at the horse's sides, and your hands on the reins – together and ask the horse to move off at a slow walk.

5. If it becomes apparent at this point – or even earlier – that the horse is going to be a handful and that you're not quite prepared to manage its high jinks, don't feel shy about asking someone to lead you for the first few minutes. Horses that haven't been exercised for a while – such as neglected private animals or hack horses that have been rested because of injury or lack of business – are quite likely to act up, usually out of high spirits rather than ill temper. If you feel at all anxious, put common sense ahead of bravado and save yourself a possible fall by being led or by dismounting and lungeing the horse, if necessary, to get the kinks out. (See page 135 for lungeing advice.) If neither alternative seems possible, stay aboard but take things very easily. Ride the horse on a relatively loose rein – being ready to pick up contact if the animal shows signs of bolting – and be very gentle with your aids. Instead of applying leg pressure, for instance, simply *think* 'walk' or 'trot' and chances are that the horse will respond. If things still look bad and there is no ring to contain your fiery steed, ask for another horse or don't ride.

6. Use a schooling area if possible for the first few minutes of your ride. If there is no fenced-in area, aim for an open, level piece of ground and work in a large circle. While you are walking the horse, which you should do for at least the first five minutes, see how he responds to more or less contact on the reins and establish the proper amount to

keep him responsive to your signals for turning and halting but not resistant.

7. The trot is the best gait at which to test a horse, so once you have your bearings, put the horse into a steady trot. It may take a couple of turns around the ring to get the gait as steady and rhythmic as you like, but don't give up. There's no point in trying anything else until you and the horse have reached a good working relationship in both directions at this gait. If the horse seems to be pulling on the reins, indicating that his weight is on the forehand rather than the hindquarters where it should be, work him at the sitting trot, bringing him to a halt every so often and even backing up once in a while.

8. Once you have figured out the trot working the full circumference of the school, trot half the school and in occasional small circles to see whether the horse 'bends' properly. Work on collecting and extending the gait, and alternate your route once in a while so that the horse doesn't anticipate your commands.

9. Once in a while you may come across a horse with more gaits than just a walk, trot and canter – or with gaits that seem to be somewhere in between the basic three. Some horses have a long walk or slow gait that involves trotting with the forelegs and walking behind; it is a peculiar gait that one cannot rise to but over long distances it is efficient and comfortable. Some horses have a natural singlefoot, a four-beat gait in which each foot hits the ground at a different time.

10. After ten minutes or so at the trot, try a canter in one direction and then in the other. If the horse takes the wrong lead, although you have given the appropriate aid, stop him and start again until you get the correct lead. (Remember that some horses have been trained to obey different aids.) If the horse seems very strong and you are planning to hack out for the rest of the hour, you might think twice about cantering on the bridle path where he is likely to get even stronger.

11. When you are outside the schooling area, the horse should have your respect enough not to take you for a ride you won't enjoy. But don't take chances. Don't gallop, jump fences or canter down steep hills – and be sure to walk the last mile home so that the horse is completely cooled out when you get back to the stable. If the day is hot and the horse is still wet from the exertion, you should offer to untack him, sponge him off with cool water and walk him on a lead shank until he is completely dry. Anyone who brings a hot horse back from a ride will be considered something a good deal less than a horseman by the stable management and could well be charged a (justifiable) penalty fee.

5
The Responsibilities

The list of responsibilities faced by the average horse owner seems endless – from the health and well-being of the horse to the maintenance of the stable in which the animal lives. The horseless rider, by comparison, is a blithe spirit who can sleep late on rainy mornings while others muck out boxes or tote bales of hay and whose letterbox is blissfully free of bills from farriers, feed stores and veterinarians. But every rider has some responsibilities – to himself, to the horse and to the others in whose company he rides – for the sake of both pleasure and safety. Being alert to potential danger or discomfort is the first step in avoiding problems, but it isn't the whole story. Knowing how to behave in certain situations will help to prevent trouble or at least keep it from getting worse. This chapter, then, is devoted to the rules of riding behaviour, the handling of difficult horses, first-aid in emergencies and some of the legal aspects of horselessness.

The art of horsemanship is an ancient one, and there are more rules, regulations, formalities and traditions connected with it than with almost any other sport. But if you remember that chivalry – another art in which proper behaviour and etiquette play a great role – derives from the French word for horse, it may not be surprising to find that what follows are a series of do's and don'ts for those who ride.

School Etiquette

At a glance, there isn't much involved in riding in an enclosed school area, but in practice, especially if there are other people in the school, there is a certain form to follow if order is to be kept where chaos can easily erupt. First of all, even when you are alone, it behoves you to display good horsemanship by keeping your mount well into the corners as you circle rather than cutting them, and to use discipline as you ride so that the horse will know you mean business. A horse that takes advantage of the informal, uncaring rider by heading into the centre of the school without being asked or by repeatedly taking the wrong lead at the canter will be no pleasure for the next rider. So when you are in the school, keep on the edges of the school unless you intend to make a circle or some other deliberate movement. Pay attention to your diagonals at the trot and to your leads at the canter, for the sake of the horse's education as well as your own. Remember that this area is called a school – and a school it should be considered, a classroom in which the horse should be encouraged to do his best at all times. Loose-reining is all right if it is part of the educational or cooling-out process but not if it is done carelessly.

The usual programme for a schooling session begins with the walk for a few minutes in both directions and then a good working trot, first in one direction and then the other. Once a steady pace is achieved, you can work on extending along the length of the school and collecting in the corners, but don't attempt this during every round. The horse will quickly pick up the habit of speeding up on the straightaway (which may not be correct extension in any case, since the number of strides should remain the same and only the strides themselves should lengthen) and slowing down or even breaking pace at the ends of the arena. Make half-schools (using half the area) and smaller circles or figures of eight occasionally to make sure that the horse has his hindquarters in gear and is sufficiently bent to make a smooth circle without ballooning out or cutting a corner. (Don't forget to change diagonals as you change direction.)

At the canter, make sure you start out on the correct lead (left lead going counterclockwise; right lead clockwise) and that you work on your inside and outside aids. Keep your hands level if you are using both hands, not one raised above the other, your legs in the proper position and your balance over the centre of the horse's balance. The whole point of the lead is that the horse can maintain balance while turning; counter-cantering (cantering on the wrong lead) will only invite a fall unless it is done by someone who knows what he's doing, such as schooling a horse to make a flying change of leads. When you practise halts or changes of gait, do so at different points of the area each time, preferably away from the entrance so that the horse won't get into the habit of stopping there whether you want him to or not.

If you are alone, you may, of course, set your own pattern, changing direction and pace when you like. But when there are other people riding, you will have to be alert to what they are doing and make your routine conform to theirs to keep confusion to a minimum. If other people are trotting in one direction, don't try to canter in the other without asking permission (especially if the other horses are hard to handle or are ridden by beginners). If you wish to walk while others are trotting, keep to the inside rather than on the rail. If, conversely, you want to trot or canter while others are moving more slowly, move in their direction but keep to the outside; if anyone is on the rail in front of you, call out 'Rail, please!' to signal that you are coming past. If that person doesn't move, don't scream and yell but circle or otherwise attempt to avoid the horse in front without letting your horse know that anything is out of order. If everyone is cantering and your horse's stride is longer or faster, don't run up on the rumps in front of you but call for the rail or make a circle to avoid a collision. A rule of thumb to follow: you are responsible for the horses ahead of you, not behind, and if they don't (or can't) move at your request, give them right of way. Another rule to keep in mind: if you are schooling your horse using voice commands, keep your voice low when others are in the area or you will confuse other horses or riders. I have often been in a school while lessons are going on and without thinking have obeyed the verbal instructions of the teacher when they weren't directed at me at all. What's worse is having your *horse* obey those commands, breaking into a trot when the teacher calls out to his students

A group lesson in an indoor school. In the foreground the instructor has set up a low vertical fence after a series of poles, which have been arranged so that the horse will trot in an even-strided, steady approach to the obstacle

even though you're trying to stay at a walk. If you find yourself in a similar situation, 'auditing' a class when you're riding on your own, you should do whatever the instructor suggests – stay out of the way or change direction – since he may be working with beginners who don't know the rules.

If you feel that you have been going in one direction long enough, suggest to the other riders that they change direction so that you can do so as well. But don't just turn around and run into them. If you want to practise halting or backing up, or if you wish to stop to adjust a stirrup or tighten the girth, don't do so in the path of other horses but move into the centre of the school or to some area where horses are not travelling. If you want to practise a special movement, such as a leg-yield or a turn on the haunches, be sure that the path is clear and that your horse won't interfere with others.

Should your horse act up, kicking out or bucking, stay calm and settle him down as quickly as possible. In a confined area nearby horses are all too likely to take another animal's disobedience as an excuse for a general riot. If another horse acts up while you are riding, keep a firm rein and anticipate disobedience in order to stop it before it starts. Some horses have a real antipathy to others, so keep those animals separated if at all possible. A dun mare I ride regularly is convinced that a fellow school horse (well-named Jughead) is out to kill her, and she stops dead in her tracks if he comes within twenty feet of her. (She has reason: even his groom admits that he would rather fight than eat.) The only solution is for me to tell his rider, whoever that may be, to keep him at a good distance no matter what. Horses that kick are occasionally made to wear red ribbons in their tails but not always, so it is up to the rider (or the stable manager) to be sure that everyone knows about this vice before they learn in a more painful way.

If a horse bolts or throws its rider, stop your horse and remain standing until the runaway has stopped or until the rider has remounted. Such an event will excite and alarm everyone and it may take a few moments of walking quietly to get the atmosphere back to normal.

If you are jumping in the ring while others are working on the flat, you will have to be especially careful to make sure your course is clear before you start. If you find that someone is in front of or behind the jump as you head towards it, simply circle and try again. In a school full of beginners, you may discover that the other riders aren't exactly sure what a gate or an oxer is, so don't be impatient. Explain what you want and be as cooperative as you expect them to be. Don't expect too much of your horse in this situation, however. If there are several riders around, a well-schooled horse should be able to mind his business (or yours, rather), but some horses are easily distracted, especially if they must weave around other animals while keeping a steady pace on a course of jumps. It is up to you to reassure him and keep him under control.

Road Etiquette

In rural parts of the country, bridle path riding is just that, but, unfortunately, as humans expand their populaton, they also expand the network of roads, and all too often riding in suburban and urban areas means road riding – at least for part of the time. In many places it will be necessary to ride along metalled roads or to cross them in order to get to bridle ways, and even in some rural areas, it is often a good idea for riders to use roads rather than fields. In the spring farmers resent riders who trample across ploughed and seeded fields, and in the autumn the hunting season can be as dangerous for horse and rider as it is for game. And so, before we get to the bridle path or park, let's cross the road.

Macadam or concrete are fine for rubber tyres but not for horses' feet, and if there is a soft shoulder wide enough to walk on, do so. Pounding on a metalled road at a trot or canter is not only hard on a horse's natural shock absorbers but it's also a risky business since the surface invites skidding, especially if one tries to make a sudden turn or halt. Horse owners who ride regularly on the streets usually take the precaution of having their animals shod with borium calks on their shoes for grip and leather pads to help absorb the pounding, but hire establishments may not take these expensive precautions. Unless you know that the horse is shod properly, keep to a walk on metalled roads at all times. Make sure that you are wearing protective gear even if your horse isn't. A hard hat – the kind used for jumping – is an extremely good idea, and should be considered as much a part of the riding uniform as a motorcyclist's helmet is part of his outfit. One man I know rented a horse from a stable in the heart of the city and while crossing a street on the way to the park, the horse shied for some reason and the man was thrown and knocked unconscious. When he came to, he looked up and saw the sign for an undertakers. It took him a few anxious moments to realize that he was really alive!

Most horses that are ridden regularly in traffic become accustomed to it, which means getting used to loud noises, blinking lights, blowing papers, cans, bottles and all kinds of distraction. Although you can assume that a public stable near a road will offer you a horse that has become street-wise, you shouldn't take chances, which means that you should keep the horse under complete control at all times. An inexperienced horse may shy or refuse to negotiate such threatening obstacles as bridges and even an experienced horse can become alarmed if he lacks confidence in his rider. It is usually a good idea to ride with other people, not only for help in case of accident but also because the presence of other animals will have a calming effect on your own mount. If you are in a group, however, don't ride abreast down the middle of the street, but ride single file along the same side. No matter how sure of yourself or your horse you are, never take any oncoming vehicle for granted and always prepare yourself for the unexpected. Most drivers will slow down and behave courteously, but some won't, either because they don't realize the danger or because they take a sadistic delight in scaring horses. Be sure to thank any driver who slows down or stops.

Take particular care in crossing streets to watch for traffic and to gauge its speed as well as to note the condition of the road before you cross. If you start to cross and a car appears, it is usually safer to keep going rather than to attempt a turn or a halt. If you are in a group, the leader should stand in the road, holding up traffic with their hand, until everyone is safely across. If traffic is heavy and your horse is nervous, it may be wiser to dismount and lead him, putting yourself between the horse and the cars. It goes without saying that you should obey traffic signs just as any other driver must and use hand signals whenever necessary.

Bridle Path Etiquette

Once you reach a nice, unpaved road or bridle path, your troubles aren't entirely over, but life will be somewhat simpler. You must remain in constant control, of course, for even the calmest of horses can always shy or bolt, but at least you aren't

Riding along bridle paths is not as formal as showing and a good deal more relaxing, considered by many to be the best possible way to view the countryside

likely to run into lorries or cars. Motorbikes, however, have begun to make inroads onto bridle paths, but your most likely companions will be other animals. If you do come across other riders on the trail, be sure that your own horse is moving at a similar or slower pace. Since horses are herd animals by nature, one horse galloping past a group of walking horses can cause a stampede, especially if the riders in the group are beginners. If the trail is narrow and you wish to pass, call out 'Passing, please!' before you barge ahead. You have the right of way and the rider being passed must move over. As you pass, don't use your crop or whip since it may startle other horses; if you must give your horse something more than simple leg pressure to move it faster, use the crop on the side away from the other horses so they can't see it. If you are being passed and the path is very narrow, move your horse's hindquarters off the path.

If you encounter a dog along the way, slow to a walk and ride past without much more than a 'go home' to the dog. Most dogs will give up barking once you have passed 'their' property line, since they tend to be territorial. If you come across the rare dog who may attack a horse, keep going and make a note to avoid that route in the future, or plan to carry a water pistol (filled only with water, please). Horses will usually treat the presence of other animals – cattle, sheep and such – without much more than a second glance and you should behave in the same way. Although many people enjoy taking their dogs along with them when they ride, it's not a good idea for the horseless rider to do so, unless the animals know each other and you know that the route you are going to take is not lined with other dogs, chaseable rabbits and similar attractions (or hazards) for your pet. When in doubt, leave your dog at home. Loose dogs around a stable can be a nuisance, barking at horses, fighting with each other and generally getting in the way.

If you are riding with a group of riders, make sure that everyone is prepared ahead of time for a change of pace. When there is a beginner or timid rider in the group who may not wish to canter or gallop, don't bolt off and expect his horse to remain walking. Either pick a spot where the beginner's horse may stand quietly as your circle around him, or ride on ahead and canter back toward the standing horse. When you ride in single file, keep at least one horse's length between each horse. A horse that walks too close to the one ahead is likely to stumble because it can't see where it's going or isn't paying attention to its rider. Tailgaiting is also a good invitation for a swift kick. Don't hold branches aside for a rider who is following you; because of the distance between the horses, the branch will probably swing back just in time to knock the rider behind you out of the saddle.

If you know or suspect that the horse you are riding is likely to shy at this or that, don't ride in front but let the other horses go first. Many spooky horses will follow another animal past a frightening object that it would take an hour to pass on its own. Although riding in groups may be an advantage in this situation, don't get carried away in conversation or let your attention stray from your own horse. As on the roads, ride defensively, anticipating trouble and keeping in control at all times. Once you know the horse you are on, this attitude can become second nature, so that hacking out will be more pleasure than work, but if you are on an unfamiliar horse going over unfamiliar terrain, don't assume that the animal is going to behave well unless he respects his rider.

Stay alert to conditions and don't attempt to canter over rocky ground, through low-hanging branches or up and down steep hills. Slow to a walk if you come upon any patches of ice, mud or sandy areas and pay special attention to holes or rocks. If you are in a field, don't just gallop across heedlessly but stay on the path around the edge. If you notice any particular hazards, point them out to other riders. If the trail takes a sharp turn downward or up, stay at a walk and don't lean back but remain over the horse's centre of gravity (the withers) to help maintain traction.

If the bridle path is owned and managed by the stable, be sure you know ahead of time where you are going, how to get back and what the boundaries are. In many areas, bridle paths are public footpaths and marked as such (often with other rules, such as 'no reckless riding') but sometimes you may find yourself having to use private property. Some property owners may be kind enough to allow riders to cross their land, but don't do so without being sure that you have their permission. A number of communities have riding associations or committees that obtain this permission and maintain good conditions, and if you are heading off into private land, it is a good idea to check with such an association ahead of time. Rude or thoughtless riders can try the patience of any landowner and if you are granted permission to cross, be sure to behave yourself. Don't allow your horse to walk on lawns or gardens, and in cultivated fields, keep to the very edge. If a crop is growing right up to the fence, stay outside the fence, and if the ground is wet, avoid the field altogether. If you come across bridges or streams, make sure that the footing is good before you proceed and that the horse is relaxed. Some animals will try to jump their way across, spilling you or getting themselves into trouble, and if you suspect any fear on the part of your animal, it may be best to dismount and lead him. (Don't pull the reins over his head, though, since he might get away and trip, and be sure to keep from under his feet if the going is tricky.) If you come to a gate, don't jump it. The footing on the other side may be poor and, more important, the horse may not be capable of negotiating an obstacle over three feet high (most gates are four feet or more). If you must open the gate, always close it after passing through.

While you are paying attention to the condition of the path and its hazards, don't forget about your horse. Whether you are riding for an hour or all day, remember that horses aren't machines and must not be overused. Films may show horses galloping over deserts all day long, but most of these running sequences were filmed over a period of days, not in an hour. If you enjoy a good canter, your horse probably will, too, but don't keep it up for more than a few minutes, and don't even try it unless you are sure that the horse is fit. Alternate gaits frequently, spending most of the time walking if you expect to be out for any length of time.

If you stop along the way for a picnic, let the horse have a rest too but don't tie him by the reins; be foresighted enough to take along a head collar and lead rope when you pack your lunch, so that the animal can enjoy grazing on his own without a bit in his mouth. If you think that the pond or stream water may be less than spring-fresh, or if the horse is in any way overheated, don't allow him to drink. Take along some water for him and allow only a few swallows. (I don't have to say, do I, that you should pack up any bits of rubbish you make along the way?)

If for any reason you have an accident or a fall while you're out, don't panic. Just be sure that you read the rest of this chapter before you go out.

On your way home, make certain that you obey the cardinal rule about walking the last mile. This will not only cool the horse down in preparation for his next ride or for a safe drink of water; it will also prevent him from becoming a stable rat, racing to the box, and it will save you some embarrassment back at the stable. Even if the horse picks up some speed knowing that he's heading home, don't give in but keep him at a walk.

Things to Take on a Trek

If you are planning to go out for more than an hour over countryside that you don't know like the back of your hand, you'll need more than just the horse. Here's what else to fit into your pack or take along with you:

1. Another horse and rider (it's always risky to ride alone).
2. A head collar and lead rope (especially if you plan to stop along the way for a rest or a picnic).
3. A knife or wirecutter (or both).
4. A water supply for you and the horse if you're going where water is scarce or suspect.
5. A blanket (you may get caught in bad weather or overnight).
6. A first-aid kit (for you and the horse).
7. A map of the area.
8. A rainproof coat.
9. A hoof pick.
10. A torch.

Special Conditions

Riding in a city park is something between road and bridle path riding. The paths are usually well kept and suitable for equine feet, but they are all too often filled with traffic in the form of joggers or bicycles, and riders should remain alert to any contingency. Onlookers ignorant of horse psychology may frighten an animal by crying out in delight or running up behind it to 'pat the nice horsie'. Children are especially dangerous in this respect. It's nice to be admired as you trot along in front of an audience, but don't let it go to your head. And don't show off your horse's speed by doing anything more than a collected canter. A horse that bolts in a park doesn't have too many directions in which to go, and bursting out into traffic or running into a pram is too much of a risk to take. Arabs and other saddle horse breeds are often 'park-trained' and this isn't just for show purposes; that high-stepping, highly controlled set of gaits is ideal for riding in parks where the extended gaits of a hunter would look (and be) rather out of place.

Riding at night is one of the most dangerous sports of all, especially if you are going across unfamiliar country or near roadways. Visibility is poor for both rider and motorist, even at twilight, and the rider should wear light-coloured clothing and carry a torch (or put a red reflector on the left stirrup and a white cloth on the horse's tail).

Riding during winter can be great fun but the special conditions do require a certain amount of caution. Borium calks should be worn by the horse on hard surfaces, but these are not necessary in soft snow, though you must stop occasionally to remove snow from the hooves to prevent a build up of icy snowballs. Don't overwork the horse so that he builds up a sweat or has difficulty breathing, and do avoid any unfamiliar spots that may actually be snow-covered ditches with poor footing. Don't bother with a special blanket for the horse unless you plan to stop for any period of time along the way, but do be sure that you wear enough protective clothing — long underwear, lined gloves and warm socks, as well as a suitable parka or down waistcoat and a warm hat.

Problem Horses

As we saw in the last chapter, every unfamiliar horse should be approached with a certain amount of caution – by asking questions about any habits he might have and by keeping alert to whatever may arise while you are in the saddle. Private horses may be highly strung, underexercised or spoiled by indulgent riders; hired horses may be temperamental as a result of poor riders or abusive treatment. Reschooling or trying on new bits or special types of tack, such as draw reins, checkreins and such, are not within the capability of the occasional rider, of course, because such things take time and expertise. Any horse ridden by several people can pick up bad habits very quickly especially if the animal is a sensitive one, and it may take a long time and a good deal of knowledge and patience to undo the damage. But even the occasional rider should know how to deal with trouble when it does occur or, even better, *before* it occurs. Knowing how to anticipate trouble takes experience, as does applying the remedy, since some of the cures for bad habits are not necessarily the most natural response. But it is worth studying the following tips before you get into the saddle so that you will have some idea about what to expect and what to do.

Bolting

Being run away with is a common fear among novice riders, and though bolting is a bad habit that should be eliminated in any school or hired horse available to a beginner, some horses may bolt out of fear or the misapplication of aids and every rider should know what to do. The first thing to remember is *not* to pull hard with the reins, for the pressure will only cause the horse to resist and run faster. Try to sit back in the saddle and lift your hands to keep his head up. If a sawing motion (giving and taking with alternate hands) does not work, your best bet is to pull up and back on one rein very firmly so that the horse is forced to make a circle. (Don't make the circle too tight or you'll risk falling off or making the horse fall over.) Gradually make the circle smaller until the horse has to slow down and you can regain control. Or you can turn the horse toward an obstacle too high to jump – the side of a barn or a huge wall – so that he will stop of his own accord. If you are on a trail where circling is impossible, you can try to lean back, weight in the saddle, and give a single sharp pull on the reins and then release. Some horses will be startled enough to let go of the bit, at which precise moment you must reclaim it. If all else fails, simply let the horse run until he tires; if you head him uphill, he'll slow down from the exertion rather quickly. Speak to the horse all the time in a firm tone, but don't yell, for that will only give him more reason to run. If the horse is running blindly into traffic or some obstacle and you fear a crash, your only recourse may be to bail out (see page 124).

Shying

Leaping sideways or ducking away from a frightening object can be the result of real fear on the horse's part or simply a manufactured fright that a sour horse uses as a ploy to unseat the unsuspecting novice. Theories about dealing with this vary, as do the causes, but the most sensible immediate response is to sit back, keeping a firm hold on the reins, and to regain your balance as quickly as you can. If the horse still seems wary of whatever it is that caused him to shy, keep him moving forward with your legs firmly on his side and constant contact on the reins, speaking reassuringly but without any hesitation on your part. Let the horse know there is nothing to worry about and don't let him sense any nervousness on your part or he'll react the same way again. Don't try to pull the horse's head away from the object, for his peripheral vision will enable him to see it anyway. If he is truly frightened, let him look at the thing and see that there is nothing to fear; dismount if necessary and, holding the reins tight under his jaw, walk him by. If you are riding with someone else whose horse seems calm, have that horse precede you. If you have a feeling that your horse is refusing to move ahead out of stubbornness, do whatever you can to get him to proceed – even circling back and tricking him past the object – but do not give up, or that horse will take advantage of the next rider at this same spot.

I have found that on a windy day horses are more likely to be startled than on calm days, and I gather that this is caused by a natural equine inclination to be wary when the wind is blowing rather than the noise of rustling leaves. Wild horses use flight as their primary defence, and when the wind is coming strongly from one direction, they have to remain on alert for signs of danger since they will not be able to sense it against the wind. Rather than refuse to ride on a windy day, you need only be prepared for the possibility and keep a reassuring voice and firm control with legs and hands.

Bucking

A horse that bucks is probably doing so out of high spirits rather than nastiness, although bucking can be caused by a sharp tap with the crop, fear or a foreign body under the saddle. Whatever the reason, you can feel a buck coming on when the horse's head drops down and his hindquarters rise beneath you. Immediately pull the horse's head up and sit back. Although sitting forward may come more naturally for you or be unavoidable if the buck is already in process, do your best to get back in the saddle and keep a firm grip on the reins, pulling up rather than down. Keep your legs strong on his sides to force him ahead. A horse whose head is up in the air and who is moving forward cannot buck. If the buck was caused by high spirits you might consider lungeing him before going out on the trail or giving him a session in the ring to use up some of the excess energy. If the source of trouble is a badly fitting bridle or saddle, check for discomfort and remedy it. A horse that bucks out of bad temperament in an effort to dislodge his rider will need reschooling by an experienced rider, but one that bucks out of fear or pain may just need reassuring.

Rearing

This is a dangerous vice, since it is possible for the horse to fall over on top of the rider; even without falling, the horse's neck can hit the rider in the face. There are several schools of thought on the subject, but all experts agree that a horse with a tendency to rear should be handled only by an experienced rider. If a horse should rear up under you, the first thing to do is to get his head down and move him ahead. You may find it easier to lean forward, grab some mane, and pull down as hard as possible with one or both reins; other experts recommend trying to slide one rein beneath the stirrup and pull as hard as possible using the stirrup as a pulley; yet another suggests leaning back, letting go of the reins, and urging the horse forward. Whatever method you use, don't pull on the reins if you lean back for you'll probably force the horse over on top of you.

Wheeling

This is similar to shying in that a horse will suddenly change direction and unseat the rider. This can occur during a canter or gallop, going into a jump or when a horse rears, and the only warning the rider gets is when one shoulder drops below its normal level, giving the horse sufficient balance to wheel around without falling. Here again, prevention is the best medicine; keep contact with the horse's mouth and keep your balance over his centre of gravity, with your legs firmly in position to discourage disobedience If you have any reason to suspect that a horse is going to give you trouble, you should be prepared for it, especially if the animal has any aversion to jumping or to a particular point on the trail. General nervousness, signaled by tail-swishing, head-tossing and such, may be a sign that something more troublesome is about to erupt.

The following vices aren't as serious as the one I've just described, but they are bad habits that can interfere with a comfortable ride. Horses that kick, graze along the trail, pull and are otherwise difficult to control, can cause accidents as easily as ones that buck and rear.

Kicking

Horses that kick are bad-mannered and people who own them should be sure that everyone knows it, either by verbal warning or by tying a red ribbon to the horse's tail. A horse that kicks at people should be given a wide berth, as should any unfamiliar horse who might be startled by a sudden move behind him. Some horses reserve their kicks for other horses and these should be put at the end of a trail ride or otherwise prevented from getting their hindquarters into the range of other animals. If a horse lowers his head and flattens his ears, a kick may be in the offing; pull the horse's head up and turn him to avoid trouble or simply move ahead. If you are riding in company with a kicker, make sure that you don't ride up close behind him (not a good idea in any case, regardless of a horse's habits).

Grass-Eating

A horse that constantly stops to eat grass along the trail can be prevented from doing so by a strong, alert rider but can cause a beginner enormous frustration and even an occasional fall over the horse's head. If you suspect that your horse is more interested in nibbling than in getting exercise, keep a firm hand on the reins to keep his head high, and keep him moving forward with your legs.

Pulling

A horse that is heavy on the forehand and seems determined to pull your arms out of their sockets is a puller and needs reschooling if that habit is to be broken. These horses are really using their rider's strength as a fifth leg, to give support that should really be coming from their hindquarters. If you've got a puller and want to enjoy your ride, you can save your arms by trying a few tricks of your own. Keep the horse moving ahead but let go of the reins suddenly; once you have removed the support, he may be surprised into letting you have control of the bit. If the pulling continues, lift your hands up to keep his head raised and maintain strong impulsion with your legs to get his weight back on his hindquarters where it belongs. As you ride, stop from time to time and make the horse back up. Use your back to brace yourself rather than letting your arms take the brunt of the pressure. You won't be able to change the horse's habit in an hour, but you'll have a more comfortable ride.

Stargazing

A horse that carries his head high to avoid contact with the bit can be difficult to control. Try riding the horse in circles at the sitting trot, allowing his haunches to swing out beyond the circle. Eventually the horse will lower his head to keep his balance and you can reclaim control of the bit.

Riders in Trouble

If a horse's high-jinks should lead to an accident, despite all your efforts to the contrary, you should be prepared to deal with the situation, whether or not you are hurt. It is always best to ride in the company of other riders or with someone looking on, just in the event of such an emergency, and you should also be able to deal with problems that arise when you are the onlooker rather than the victim. The following suggestions are in no way intended as the last word on the subject; anyone who plans to spend a lot of time around horses should be familiar with the basics of first aid – both for humans and for horses. First, humans.

Falling Off

If you find yourself completely unbalanced and heading for the ground, try to remember to go limp to avoid landing in a tense, breakable heap. If the horse is going fast, try to roll up your body so that you do not risk hitting your head or the loose arm or leg as you fall. Professional riders fall as much as anyone else and it's worth asking your instructor for advice about how to fall or even to practise falling on your own (from a chair onto a mattress or at the local gymnasium), just to make sure your reactions are automatic. Obviously, the occasional rider needn't go to these lengths, but anyone who is taking up cross-country riding or jumping would do well to learn the technique before an accident teaches you a lesson you'll never forget. Most important for all beginners and for anyone who jumps is to wear a hard hat, just in case. Everyone who rides falls off sooner or later and the sooner the better if one is going to learn to do it properly. I once had a friend in a riding class who had ridden for several years without falling off; one evening she took a tumble and instead of panicking, she jumped to her feet saying, 'Thank heavens that's over! I used to be terrified of falling off but now I know it's not as bad as I thought!'

Some falls, of course, *can* be bad, causing serious injury – especially if the horse steps or falls on the fallen rider. Don't try to hang on to the reins as you fall and do try to fall as clear of the horse as possible. Horses will do almost anything to avoid stepping on something in their path so you needn't worry about this too much unless the horse falls, too. If you are riding under supervision, the instructor or guide should be capable of giving the necessary first aid, but it's always a good idea to know some of these yourself if you plan to ride out alone or in company with someone less experienced than yourself. (See over for first-aid measures.)

Loose Horse

If you fall and your horse heads for home, you have nothing to do but to follow on shank's pony. If the horse should stop to graze, don't run after him assuming that you can catch him. Walk calmly, speak softly and carry a big bunch of attractive-looking grass to catch his attention so that he forgets he's loose. If you are riding with other people, don't have all your friends try to catch him, for that will only cause the horse to become excited and run off. If reins are dangling in front of him, he can injure himself or break the reins. Some years ago I learned a marvellous way to catch a loose horse from someone who realized that horses have a natural curiosity about anything unusual so long as it doesn't seem to threaten them. If you are trying in vain to catch an animal and buckets of oats or handfuls of grass aren't effective or available, pay no attention to the horse but go off in a direction away from him –staying close enough so that he can see what you're doing. Sit down, fool around with a stone or whatever and make interesting noises, concentrating thoroughly on that stone. Before long the horse's curiosity should get the better of him and he'll try to figure out what's so interesting. Don't make a move in his direction until he is standing right over you, and then – quickly but deliberately – catch hold of the rein or halter and he's yours – disappointed perhaps, but definitely yours.

Injured Riders

If you do get hurt in a fall or otherwise and you are out on the trail alone, your best bet is to take it easy until you know that you can move without doing yourself further injury. Most horses will find their way home and the sight of a riderless horse will galvanize everyone at the stable into action on your behalf. If the horse does not leave you, don't worry about catching him until you are safely on your feet and can manage it. Lie still until you get your wind and your wits back and can determine whether or not you have broken anything or have simply been bruised. Only when you are calm – even if you are in pain – should you make a move to get help.

If you are with a rider who gets injured, you should, of course, try to get expert help, but you may have to apply first aid as well if the injury is serious. If someone is knocked unconscious, immediately make sure that he or she can breathe; using your hand or your crop, open the mouth and clear it of any dirt or other debris and hold the head so that there is an air passage to the throat. Apply artificial respiration if breathing is not obvious – mouth-to-mouth or mouth-to-nose – sealing off all breathing passages except where your mouth is and breathing for the victim (fifteen to twenty breaths a minute). Watch to be sure that the chest rises each time you breathe out. If there is excessive bleeding, use a pressure bandage by placing a clean piece of cloth directly over the source of the bleeding and holding it firm until the bleeding stops. Don't try a tourniquet (both dated and dangerous as a form of first aid) and don't worry at this point about infection, since loss of blood is more serious. Elevate the bleeding area and treat the victim for shock, by having him or her lie down on a blanket to prevent chilling (or overheating). If you suspect a fracture, do not move the victim unless you have to and until you have immobilized the injured area with a splint of some sort.

If you or another rider with you gets kicked or bitten by a horse, wash the injured area with cold water to reduce pain and to clean it, and treat as you would any other injury, getting medical attention if it seems necessary.

Severe sprains should be treated like fractures; a minor sprain should be given a cold-water bath to reduce pain and swelling and then bandaged (for support) and elevated. Don't be too brave and try to deny that a sprain or a bruise hurts; I once had my ankle kicked by a horse and treated it like a bruise by simply hoping that the pain would go away. It wasn't until a week later, when the bruise didn't seem to be healing, that my mother insisted on an X-ray, which revealed that the tibia bone had, in fact, been dealt a hairline fracture.

One school of thought recommends that you should get back on a horse the minute you fall off, on the theory that you will eliminate whatever psychological damage the accident may have caused. There may be some truth to this with beginners who are not seriously injured, but sometimes the pain caused by remounting your horse is worse than staying safely on the ground. The jarring that a few more minutes in the saddle can cause may also have serious consequences if an injury has occurred. Sometimes injuries are not immediately apparent. After one of my falls, I got right back on the horse and finished up my hour in the saddle; then I drove home, took a cold bath and went to bed. When I awoke the next morning, I couldn't move my knee, since the muscles and tendons had discovered during the night of inactivity that they had been severely sprained. I had to wait at least three weeks before I could ride, though I found – to my delight – that my reluctance to cause pain by jarring the knee kept my legs in the proper position after I was back in the saddle again. Nevertheless, it isn't worth doing yourself physical damage just for the sake of psychological health, no matter what the old wives and horsemen say.

Horses in Trouble

If an equine accident or sudden illness should occur and neither the owner nor an expert is available, you may find yourself having to cope with the situation on your own. The first and most important step to take if you have any doubt about whether the symptoms are serious is to get back to the stable as fast as possible and to see that a veterinarian is called. If the stable manager or the horse's owner is not around, call a vet yourself. Every stable should have the vet's number posted prominently (usually inside the first-aid kit or on the medication shelf in the stable) but if you have any trouble finding it, consult the directory or telephone information service for the nearest veterinary clinic. If the vets there do not handle large animals, they will refer you to someone who does. Follow whatever instructions you are given over the telephone and use whatever first-aid techniques seem appropriate, depending on the problem. There are several good books that outline these techniques (particularly worth reading are chapters 1 and 13 of *The Complete Book of Horse Care* by A. Fraser and F. Manolson (Pitman)), and it's worth committing these methods to memory if the books are not on hand in the stable. The most important thing to keep in mind is to reassure the horse and keep him calm to prevent the situation from getting worse.

Lameness

If your horse goes lame when you are riding, dismount immediately and check each hoof for a lost shoe, an imbedded stone or some other foreign object. Don't check only the foot you think is causing the problem; it isn't easy to diagnose lameness correctly unless you are an expert. If you do see something in the foot that is causing pain, try to remove it as gently as possible with a hoof pick, but if you can't dislodge it wait until you can get some help. Often the removal of the object will improve the situation enormously, but don't just remount and ride off into the hills until you are certain that there is no further pain. If you have any doubts, lead the horse back to the stable and either ask for another horse or call it quits for the day.

If there is no obvious cause for the lameness, leave it to an expert or a vet to diagnose the source of the trouble and put the horse away in the box or paddock until the expert arrives. Lameness can be caused by any number of injuries or illnesses – from pulled muscles to digestive troubles to inborn weaknesses –and treatment will vary considerably, depending on the cause. Rest and recuperation will cure many ills, but some horses may require special medications or even surgery. Your primary responsibility as rider is to notice that there is a problem, to get help as quickly as possible, and to become a pedestrian immediately.

Accidents

If a horse should fall or be injured in some way, approach the animal with caution, since you may put yourself into danger if he is upset or afraid, or flailing around trying to get up or away. Speak reassuringly to him, try to figure out what the injury is, and get help immediately. If first aid is required, see the box for some hints, but consult a veterinary manual or an experienced rider for further information. If you are alone on the trail, you may have to leave the horse to get help if he cannot be led home. Don't tie him or he may cause himself further injury. If the animal has been caught in wire, you should obviously try to get him free, but if you can't rescue him yourself from mud, a ditch or some more complicated situation, call the local fire or police station for assistance. If an electrical wire is involved, don't touch the horse or the wire (or any water that may be nearby). Stay away and call the electricity or telephone company.

Illness

Most hired horses are relatively healthy and the rider is, in any case, rarely in a position to determine whether a symptom exists or not, let alone a serious illness. But in the interest of developing a degree of horsemanship and for the sake of the conscientious horse-sitter, I have included a very brief summary of symptoms to note and first-aid techniques to master.

Colic is the most common ailment that requires first aid at home before the veterinarian comes, so it is worth your learning its symptoms and what to do about them. If a horse lies down and rolls in obvious pain, you must keep him on his feet and walking constantly; intestinal twisting or torsion may be aggravated or caused by the rolling, and walking the horse will prevent this and also help distract the animal from his pain. A veterinarian may treat the horse by feeding it mineral oil or some concoction to loosen the bowel or he may inject a muscle relaxant, but these remedies should not be undertaken by a novice.

Because it is difficult for anyone but an expert to diagnose the actual illness, your responsibility will be to notice the symptoms and get help. The following symptoms deserve a call to the vet:

Refusal to eat or drink for 24 hours
Repeated coughing
High temperature (over 103°F)
Shivering or excessive sweating for no obvious reason
Diarrhoea or constipation for more than 12 hours
Frequent lying down and rolling
Persistent lameness.

Legal Considerations

Being aware of the potential danger in working around horses and knowing how to handle emergency situations should keep accidents and injury to a minimum. But, as any horseman will tell you, accidents can happen even in the best of all worlds, and any horseless rider should understand the legal responsibilities involved in riding other people's horses.

In general, the owner of any animal has what is known as a 'duty of care' to anyone who comes in contact with it. This

First-aid for Equine Accidents

Open Wounds

1. Abrasions – surface scrapes or sores. Clean the area with water or a mild saline solution and keep it free of flies and dirt; do not bandage or use disinfectants, and do not allow any tack to come into contact with the affected area. Medication or veterinary attention should not be necessary.
2. Incision or puncture wounds. Clean with water or saline solution but do not bandage. If the wound appears to be deep, get a vet to look at it, since infection can set in if the skin heals over the injury. The vet will probably give a tetanus shot as well as antibiotics.
3. Lacerations or tears. These may require stitching, which should be done by a vet. You may clean the area if the horse can be handled but don't use disinfectants, only warm water, and try to pull any loose flaps of skin back into place.
4. Excessive bleeding. If the bleeding doesn't stop after a minute or two or if the blood is bright red and spurting, you will have to apply a pressure bandage to stop it. Put a clean piece of cloth around or on the area and hold it tight until the bleeding stops. Keep the bandage in place until the vet arrives and don't bother with a tourniquet, which will only complicate matters.

Strains and Sprains

These are injuries to muscles and tendons and may be caused by overwork or accident. Mild injuries can be treated with an alcohol rub or a mild liniment but more serious injuries should get a vet's attention. Keep the affected area cool (by using a hose) and avoid swelling; only after the area has cooled and stopped swelling should one apply heat treatments to increase circulation and promote healing.

Bruises and Fractures

These are injuries to the bone and may, of course, be very serious, requiring a vet's attention. Some fractures are obvious and some are not, so don't try to diagnose the problem yourself. Keep the horse calm and relaxed in a darkened enclosure until the vet arrives. If the horse is trying to move about, you may have to apply a splint to keep an injured leg immobile. Wrap a thick cloth or pillow around the leg and tape it as securely as possible, supporting the leg by taping sticks or poles to opposite sides of the pillow.

In case of accident:
1. Don't hesitate to call a vet.
2. Don't apply medications without instruction from a vet (tranquilizers are especially dangerous to a horse in pain).
3. Don't panic but reassure the animal as much as possible to keep him calm (a quiet, dark place makes a good waiting room).
4. Don't try to diagnose anything and treat it yourself unless the injury is obviously minor.
5. Don't approach an injured animal except with the utmost caution.

common law means that if the owner can be proved negligent in a situation that results in injury or death, he is liable for damages. A horse owner, therefore, must provide customers or borrowers with a horse that is safe and suitable, with regard to the abilities of the rider, and he also has the responsibility to inform the rider if the animal has any potentially dangerous characteristics. The liability is also extended to third parties – such as anyone using a road or highway if a horse is known to shy in traffic and if the animal has been entrusted to someone not competent to handle it on the road. (Motorists also have a duty of care to riders when they pass a horse on the road.) If it can be proved that the rider acted negligently in handling the horse on the road, he too might be liable for damages. As for accidents that might take place around a stable area, the Occupiers Liability Act of 1957 provides that the occupier of the premises owes a duty of care to anyone visiting to see that the visitor will be reasonably safe in using the premises for which he is invited or permitted. (The Act requires occupiers to insure themselves against liability for negligence as well.)

Many riding stables will put up signs saying 'Ride at Your Own Risk' or something similar, and some will even insist that the customer sign a release agreeing to take responsibility if injury should occur. According to the Unfair Contract Terms Act 1977, such signs or releases do not necessarily relieve the owner of the stable of liability if negligence can be proved. An owner who allows someone to hire a horse without properly warning him of the animal's potentially dangerous habits may be found negligent. If a rider is warned of any such habit, however, and signs a release agreeing to take the risk, then he cannot legally complain if an injury should result. (This law covers only horse owners who are in the business; private owners lending animals to friends are covered by the common law described above.)

In spite of laws, however, my recommendation to horseless riders is that unless negligence is obvious and provable, you should approach every horse and every ride with the idea that the responsibility is your own. If you borrow or hire an animal that has been presented as a gentle, safe creature, and it explodes quite unexpectedly, the lender may be negligent in not having warned you, but you may be at fault for having inadvertantly mistreated it – by giving it a confusing signal, or forcing it to do something it refuses to do, such as take a fence, go through a stream or under a bridge. Sometimes the cause is something that could not have been foreseen by either horse or rider: a bee sting, a thoughtless motorist or a suddenly awakened memory of something frightening in the horse's past experience. Even if a piece of tack breaks or slips while you are riding, you should count yourself at fault for not having checked everything before you started out. If you are a real beginner and the lender knows that, you may have some justification for placing the fault with him if sufficient precautions were not taken. But anyone who mounts a horse must realize that the possibility of falling off or otherwise being injured is always there. If it's money for damages that you want, there are more pleasant ways to get it. In the meantime, I can only repeat what it says in most stables I know:

RIDE AT YOUR OWN RISK

6
Making the Most of
Your Ride

Sooner or later, usually sooner, the average horseless rider begins to get restless. The hacks at the local stable aren't much of a challenge anymore; the instructor has taught you the basics but you want to explore different types of equitation on more highly schooled horses; you've been bitten by the bug of competition; or you want a chance to try some advanced kinds of equestrian activity. But you still have the same old limitations of time, money and horselessness. What to do? Believe it or not it is perfectly possible to improve the quality of each ride without completely changing your lifestyle (if you're prepared to do *that*, skip right to chapter 9 for advice), and even without changing stables. Here are some tips.

Improving the Horse

If the horses at your stable are nice, plodding animals that have lost their charm for you, don't despair and don't start looking elsewhere . . . yet. Any horse, regardless of conformation or past experience, will benefit from a change of pace, and it is definitely worth trying to change that pace for them, if you can convince the stable manager to let you do so. If you are a regular customer, ask if you may be allowed to school one of the horses in some new discipline. Study the books on dressage, for example, or elementary jumping, and learn what is involved in training a horse. You may have to adjust your schedule to a time when the stable facilities are not busy, and you may even have to get some new equipment to start, but perseverance will usually win out. A dressage whip and access to a school are all you'll need for dressage schooling; jumping will also demand a ring – or a level piece of ground – and a few rails and standards. If the stable management can't be convinced to invest in these or to lend you some rails from which you can fashion some jumps, offer to buy the lumber and undertake to make them yourself, trading them for a few free rides. Never assume that an old horse can't learn new tricks. Some friends of mine own a nineteen-year-old pony who recently acquired a new lease on life by learning to jump low crossrails. They don't work him very hard, of course, but they swear that he acts like a seven-year-old every time he is headed in the direction of their jumping course.

Although lungeing a horse doesn't involve riding – since the lunger stands in the middle of an area while the lungee circles around him at the end of a longe or lunge line, this is a useful training technique that will benefit both horse and horseman. In addition to its value in initial training, lungeing is an excellent

Lungeing a horse – for exercise or special schooling

way to give an underexercised or overexcited animal a chance to warm up or cool down as the case may be. You can use a plain halter or a special lunging cavesson (a halter with one or three rings attached to a special noseband), attaching the swivel snap of the lunge line, a twenty-five-foot length of lightweight material (usually cotton or nylon) to the ring under the horse's jaw. You will also need a long whip to act in place of your legs as an aid, supplemented by your voice, to make the horse walk, trot, canter and stop in both directions around you. Lunged horses usually wear a lungeing surcingle or a saddle with the stirrups tied down to the girth to prevent flapping, and sometimes a bridle or a bitting rig is used instead of a halter.

Long-reining is a variation of lungeing. Two long lines are attached to the bridle, the line on the inside (near you) run through the stirrup and the outside rein brought through the outside stirrup and run around behind the horse's hocks. If you have never used a lunge line or long reins, the simplest way to learn is to watch an expert at work and then to try your hand under supervision. Long reins can also be used to train a horse to drive when the trainer walks directly behind the horse.

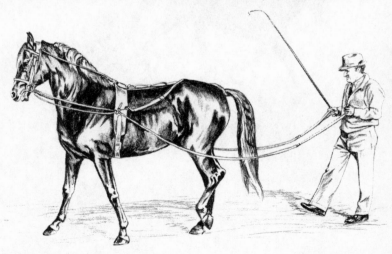

Teaching a horse to drive by using long reins. The whip is used to give cues (together with the voice) in place of the rider's legs and seat

Driving is another useful technique for the horseless rider to know, and here again the best way to learn is for someone to teach you. Many harnesses are turning up in old barns and at tack sales these days, and with a little reconditioning (or a lot, depending on the previous owner), they are perfectly useful.

Speaking of old tack, you may, as I did recently, come across an old forgotten sidesaddle. Don't just chuckle but try it on a willing animal with broad shoulders. The first time I tried I was awkwardness personified until I got a feel for the proper seat at the walk, whereupon I felt elegant and nicely balanced – until I started to trot, that is, which took a lot more practice to perfect. Frankly I never did get very good because I didn't spend enough time at it, but I had fun trying. I have no idea what the pony I rode thought of it all, but I'd be glad to try it again (even if he wouldn't), though I know I'll only do so if no one else is going to be around to watch! (See page 187 for more on the sidesaddle.)

Reschooling a difficult or spoiled horse is a great art as well as a challenge, and one that any stable manager will appreciate. If you notice that one or two of the hack horses have picked up some bad habits, offer your services as a remedial teacher. This will work only if your methods are effective, and that will take study, patience and skill, but if you are beyond the novice stage, you should be able to handle whatever comes along. (You may find R. S. Summerhays' *The Problem Horse* (J. A. Allen) especially useful.)

Most instructors I've talked with tell me that they rely on their advanced students to reschool problem horses, and it goes without saying that learning to do so is an important step toward becoming a horseman. It may also get you a few free rides, especially if your work results in savings for the horse's owner by making it unnecessary for him to get a new horse or by increasing the number of trustworthy animals in the stable. You won't be able to hang out a shingle announcing yourself as an equine psychiatrist or a fully fledged trainer until you get a couple of years of experience under your belt, but the satisfaction will be well worth the trouble.

If simple hacking is not challenging enough, try schooling the horse –
teaching it to bend properly into a turn as this rider is doing

If none of this is possible or interesting to you, you can try to persuade the stable manager into getting a new, more advanced horse, not just for yourself but for other regular customers as well. Try to get other frustrated riders to help you do the convincing; suggest that the stable might attract more clients if their stock improved. You can even look around for a horse that's for sale and offer to try it out for the stable. If you were a professional, you could get a percentage of the sale price, but perhaps you can negotiate a free ride for the service; in any event, you'd have a better horse available the next time you want one. Most public stables have a certain amount of turnover in horses; offer your services as a trial rider for the new ones. Not every ride will be a pleasure, but at least life won't be boring!

Improving the Instructor

This can be a delicate business, especially if the teacher's schedule is a busy one or if he or she is limited in ability or interest, but I've found that most instructors who care about their profession are open to new ideas presented intelligently and tactfully. As I've already said, being completely frank with your instructor is an important aspect of the entire relationship, and the time when you become frustrated by, or not altogether satisfied with, your lessons is no exception. Instead of complaining to your friends or family, tell your instructor your true feelings about the lessons and ask for advice. If you have read a new book about a particular type of riding that interests you, lend the book to your instructor and ask for comments. Suggest that you try a new direction in your own lessons – such as jumping or dressage. If your instructor thinks that you are making a mistake or getting in over your head by trying something new, he or she may be right and you should weigh the argument carefully. If the instructor isn't interested in helping you, ask for recommendations for different instructors to whom you might apply. If you're not the only student interested in something new, it might even be worth the instructor's while to get another expert to help out by giving a weekly group lesson or an occasional clinic at the stable.

You shouldn't feel embarrassed about leaving one teacher for another; be appreciative for what you have learned but remember that you are the one who's paying, and that you deserve to get something in return. The situation may be particularly touchy if you have decided to move from one instructor to another at the same stable, and this may take some political diplomacy as well as honesty, especially if your reasons for changing have more to do with personality than with riding. If the stable pays its teachers a commission rather than a straight salary, your move may have a financial as well as a personal effect on the relationship between the instructors. The only advice I can offer here is to be absolutely sure you want to make the change and to be certain that the reasons are sound enough for you to undergo whatever discomfort the change may provoke. If honesty with both instructors doesn't clear the air, you might ask the stable manager for advice or help in smoothing things over.

Another, virtually inevitable difficulty that will arise in changing instructors is that the transition will not be entirely smooth in terms of your own riding. You will be asked to unlearn some techniques or to do things that your previous teacher had trained you not to do. This will be especially true if you are attempting to learn an entirely different style of riding, but don't be tempted to argue or disobey. If you have questions or difficulty in adapting, ask the new instructor to explain what he or she is teaching and why it is different. If you understand the new technique intellectually, you should eventually be able to pass the information along to your body until your reactions become automatic.

Norman dello Joio, a young American show jumper, told me that he studied with several different trainers until he managed to arrive at what he felt was his own, most natural style. He feels that riding with a single teacher – like riding a single horse – can limit your experience, and though he was often confused at first by a new trainer, he was fortunate – or farsighted – enough to know what he wanted to learn from each one.

If your problem is simply that your instructor is too busy to give you special lessons or your schedule doesn't coincide with a different or more advanced class, you might consider the possibility of helping the teacher by giving a few beginner lessons yourself. If you show any ability in being able to help others with their riding problems, you could end up lightening your instructor's load to the extent that he or she could be free to give you the special attention you want. Learning how to teach is useful in any case, for the sake of your own riding. It is virtually impossible to spend an hour repeating 'Heels down' or 'Heads up' and to forget about your own heels and head the next time you find yourself in the saddle!

Improving the Ride

If you're becoming frustrated by the kind of riding you've been doing simply because you're in the rut of the same old school and same old bridle paths, changing horses or instructors may not answer your needs. In the next chapter we'll look at some of the competitive and advanced activities open to the horseless rider, but on a less ambitious level there are plenty of easy ways in which to make the most of the average hour's ride. First of all, if you haven't been taking lessons for a while, you will find that one or a series of sessions with a more experienced rider or an instructor will give you a new lease on your equestrian life. If you've been riding alone, try teaming up with one or two other people when you go out for a hack – or even into the school. Even watching someone else ride can teach you something, but the main difference will be in the interest that any social occasion will stimulate. Riding can be a wonderful way of meeting new people, and I've made more than a dozen close friends through a mutual interest in horses. If you meet someone who enjoys riding, ask them to join you one day for a hack through the countryside; it's not exactly as seductive as an evening looking over your etchings or as productive as a sewing bee, but it is fun and it will give your usual hour astride a new dimension. A friend of mine admits that he rides primarily for the social pleasure that it gives him; he is a fine rider who enjoys the sport for its own sake, but he is also gregarious and gets an enormous amount of satisfaction out of the company of other, like-minded people. His degree of cordial hospitality to new riders to the stable is invariably rewarded by similar hospitality when he visits other parts of the country. He finds, as I did, that his reception at a new stable – and the quality of his horse – is always far better if he knows someone who is a regular rider there.

If you have tried all the new bridle paths, all the horses and all the company, and your hour hack is still not giving you as much pleasure as you'd like, you can always pretend that you are working rather than just riding for the fun of it. I often find in travelling to new places that I get much more out of the trip if I have something to do rather than just enjoy myself. Sightseeing is fine until you have seen all the sights, but being somewhere *for a reason* can make you feel like more of a participant than a passenger. And the same goes for riding. The next time you go out hacking on old Dobbin, set yourself a schedule, whether it is to improve yourself or the horse. Make a list of things that you or the animal need to work on and set up an hour's worth of exercises to work on them. If you need a goal, pretend that you're going to enter a horse show (even better, plan to enter a horse show, see the next chapter). Here are some suggestions:

Rider Improvement
1. *To keep your heels down.* Stand up in the stirrups in a two-point seat for five minutes at the walk and trot.
2. *To develop a strong seat.* Ride at the sitting trot for five minutes or ride without stirrups at the walk, trot and canter.
3. *To develop good hands.* Ride for five minutes at the walk, alternately collecting and extending, but think *only* about your hands. Then try this at the trot.
4. *To improve your balance.* Have someone hold the horse still while you practice leaning forward and back in the saddle with your arms outstretched from the shoulder. Twist from the waist in both directions with your arms out. Ask

someone to lunge the horse for you while you ride, and drop the reins, knotting them to keep them from flapping. Work at the walk, trot and canter.

Horse Improvement
1. *Head carriage*. Work at the walk and then the trot and canter by alternately collecting the horse and extending the gaits in both directions around a ring. Change direction frequently and make your signals distinct and deliberate so that the horse is 'listening' to you. Don't overdo this; three minutes should suffice at each gait.
2. *Bending around corners*. Concentrating on making deliberate aids at turns in the ring or trail. At the trot make increasingly smaller circles, using your signals deliberately until the horse responds by bending. Weave the horse around a slalom pattern of cones or poles to develop flexibility. Concentrate on the use of your legs rather than the reins.
3. *Response to leg pressure*. Work on leg yields by making a horse move ahead on a diagonal track. Practise turns on the forehand and haunches, first by a wall or fence and then in the open.
4. *General conditioning*. To strengthen muscles, balance and surefootedness, walk and trot the horse up and down gradual slopes for a few minutes during each ride. Be sure to shift diagonals at the trot when your rise even on a straightaway.
5. *Attitude*. Make a change of scene when you can. If you are accustomed to riding in school, take the horse out hacking to relax. If you tend to hack, ride the horse for half an hour in the school to work on aids for correct leads at the canter and simply to give him the idea that he is working. I once rode an over-enthusiastic field hunter for an hour in a covered school. At first he hated the sight of the place and pretended that he was afraid of the jumps so that it took some doing to get him even into a decent trot. But after he realized that he wasn't going to get his own way and that the painted walls

and crossrails weren't going to bite him, he settled down and eventually jumped a course of small jumps that must have looked like sticks on the ground to him. His owner told me later that the following day in the field, he behaved like a gentleman for the first time, taking his fences with care and not trying to race to the front of the field.

If you have tried all that and still want more, how about forming a club? In chapter 3, I mentioned certain types of clubs open to children and adults, but there's no reason why you couldn't put together an informal group right in your own stable. Talk to some of the other regulars and suggest monthly meetings to discuss stable activities over a drink, supper, or just tea and cake. By pooling your resources, you should easily be able to afford the services of one of the many experts that travel round the country giving lectures on various aspects of riding. A quick glance at one of the horse magazines will give you some ideas for people to invite, or you can get your instructor or stable manager to help you by recommending local experts whom you may not know. Have the farrier and the veterinary surgeon speak about their specialities; ask a local show jumper or dressage coach to talk about their areas of expertise. Get one of the grooms to give a lecture on stable management or even a series of lectures on various aspects of horse care. (The clever groom might even get some of the 'students' to clean some tack or muck out a few stalls.) If one member of the group has been to a special horse show, get him or her to give a lecture about the experience. These sessions will be even more fun if you can get hold of some slides or a film to accompany the discussion. Professionally made films can be hired from various organizations (check the advertisements in the horse magazines or write to the British Horse Society), or from local colleges and universities with horsemanship programmes. Other club activities could include day trips to nearby horse shows, polo games or race tracks, dressage trials or breeding farms.

One informal club I know meets every Sunday morning at a

nearby stable to take a cross-country ride on hired horses. The only prerequisite for membership is a good deal of expertise and courage since the ride involves some tricky terrain and fences. There is no charge (beyond the fee for hiring the horse) but if anyone falls off during the ride, that person is required to buy everyone else breakfast afterwards.

The next chapter will give you ideas for competitive or advanced equestrian activities, but first how about taking a holiday – a holiday on horseback, that is? Two weeks at a pony-trekking centre can do wonders, and riding through the hills of Hungary can be a great change of pace for a rider accustomed only to the local riding schools. As horseback riding becomes increasingly popular, resorts and tourist centres begin to add riding to their attractions. A friend of mine, born in Argentina, paid a dutiful filial visit to his parents and found, to his considerable pleasure, that his home town of Buenos Aires had become a very horsy town since his childhood. He joined the local Hipoteca for the month he stayed in Argentina and rode every day on an extremely fine stallion under the tutelage of the local instructor who was, it turned out, a former member of the Argentine Equestrian Team. That, plus the fact that he was able to buy custom-made boots and a saddle – at very reasonable prices – caused his friends back home to turn pea-green with envy, but his renewed enthusiasm for the sport was enough to infect all of us as well.

Whether you travel to the continent or the New World for your equestrian holiday, you are likely to come across a horse that is wearing tack you have never seen before (except possibly at the cinema) and has been trained in a completely unfamiliar way. If you are lucky enough to find yourself aboard a Lippizaner, remember all of the dressage you ever knew and remember too that every move you make is going to mean something to the horse, even if it means nothing to you. A friend of mine once visited Spain and was given the chance to ride an Andalusian stallion. Although she knew enough not to kick the horse in the ribs or to let go of the reins to urge it forward, she was totally unprepared for the horse to canter off on the left lead when she merely lowered her head to check the position of her right stirrup!

Most of us will never get a riding opportunity such as that, but every horseless rider should be prepared for the unusual experience when it comes along. In the United States, for instance, you are likely to find yourself riding in a Western saddle at some point – in the Eastern States as well as in the 'Wild' West. Don't be nervous of the high horn at the front of the saddle; ignore it (it's for holding the rope with which you will be lassoing calves). Hold the reins (which will attach to a curb bit) very loosely in one hand as you rest your other hand on your thigh. Sit upright and keep your legs straight; relax and enjoy yourself. You needn't rise to the trot, which is called a jog and should be gentle enough to sit to, although rising is acceptable behaviour these days. Don't lean forward at the canter, which is called a lope, but stay back in the saddle. In some areas of the United States, you may find yourself facing a high-stepping horse with a very flat saddle and a set of double reins. This horse will expect you to know what saddle-seat equitation is and, if you don't, follow the instructions in the box below and remember to keep your weight back, even at the faster gaits. These horses are highly animated in front, and your weight must remain well behind their centre of balance for them to perform well. Many horses are trained to this style – not only the three- and five-gaited horses of the show ring but also the Arabs, Morgans, Tennessee Walking Horses and other flashy American breeds.

Improving Your Morale

Sometimes all it takes to make horselessness bearable is a boost to the ego. One way to give yourself a lift, even if you're stuck on the same old hack every weekend, is to visit the local tack shop and invest in a new pair of jodphurs or a jacket. The visit itself will be fun, even if you may walk out with only a new crop or a list of things to put on your Christmas list. I have always felt a great deal better in the saddle if I'm wearing a well-fitting hacking jacket (which doubles as office wear during the week),

How to Start, Stop and Turn in Any Language

The following instructions are not necessarily universal nor will they work on every horse, but they are the most common aids used these days and well worth committing to memory in case you find yourself aboard a horse that refuses to tell you who his trainer was.

1. *Balanced seat (or dressage).* *Start* by giving pressure on both sides of the horse with your calf muscles, moving your seat bones forward in the saddle, releasing slightly with the reins.

   Stop by arching your back, giving pressure on both sides of the horse with your calves, and holding the reins firm to resist forward movement.

   Turn by putting pressure at the girth on the side toward which you wish to move, putting your outside leg behind the girth and pulling gently on the inside rein (the rein facing the direction you wish to turn).

2. *Forward seat.* *Start* by applying calf pressure on both sides of the horse, leaning slightly forward and releasing pressure on the reins. Make a clucking noise if the horse doesn't respond immediately and apply more pressure with the legs, using a crop if necessary.

   Stop by applying pressure with the legs and resisting with the hands, saying 'whoa'.

   Turn by applying pressure at the girth on the inside leg, using a direct or indirect rein on the side toward which you wish to move, keeping the outside rein steady.

3. *Stock seat (Western).* *Start* by giving pressure just behind the girth with both legs, leaning slightly forward and moving the rein hand ahead to release pressure. (If that doesn't work, give a kick with both heels behind the girth or on the horse's shoulders.)

   Stop by saying 'whoa', leaning slightly back and taking up the reins until you make contact with the mouth.

   Turn by laying the reins (which are held in one hand only) on the side of the neck opposite the direction you wish to turn. Apply some pressure by pulling your hand across the neck if the horse doesn't respond right away; you can also try leaning slightly in that direction.

4. *Saddle (or park) seat.* *Start* by applying pressure with your legs at the girth, saying 'walk', leaning back slightly, and, with your hands held relatively high, release pressure on the horse's mouth. If the horse doesn't respond, kick lightly with both heels and use a whip to reinforce the aid.

Stop by releasing pressure on the reins and leaning slightly forward, arching the back and applying pressure at the knees. If the horse does not respond, lower your hands and apply rein pressure with a mild jerk (not a steady pull) to get its attention and say 'whoa'.

Turn by using a direct rein on the side toward which you wish to turn, holding the outside rein steady and applying pressure at the girth with the inside leg.

Stirrup Lengths

When you sit in the saddle with your legs relaxed and hanging down straight, the bottom of the stirrup should be:

1. At the anklebone or just below for *balanced seat*.
2. 1 to 1½ inches above sole of boot for *stock seat (Western)*.
3. Just above sole of boot for *saddle seat*.
4. Just above anklebone for *forward seat*.
5. Just below anklebone for *dressage*.

but just sitting in a store entirely filled with horsy stuff is a nice way to spend time if not money. There is always someone there who's got time for talk, and for some reason people in saddlery shops seem to be far more patient than most salesmen about explaining new products or letting you try on things. During these conversations I've met other customers interested in discussing local stables.

If you come into a windfall and have some extra cash to get rid of, one of the most satisfying purchases can be a saddle of your own. Don't think that only horse owners need saddles. Most of the truly dedicated horseless riders have saddles of their own and this is not simply because they make attractive conversation pieces in the living-room. Although it is crucial that a saddle does not cause a horse discomfort, saddles are not like shoes from the horse's point of view; in other words, most horses can wear many different saddles. Surprising as it may seem, it is important that the saddle fit the rider properly, and most instructors I've had were delighted to learn that I could bring my own. Although I can't truthfully say that owning a saddle is as good as owning a horse, it gave me peculiar satisfaction to install a saddle rack in my 'tack room' (which most people mistakenly think is my study) and it gives me pleasure just to look at it from time to time as I sit at my typewriter. Soon after I got it, a colleague of mine – a former cowboy and polo player from California – gave me a can of leather conditioner. 'How often do you use it,' I asked him, knowing that he still owned his old stock saddle, though it hadn't touched the back of a horse for some years. 'Oh every night at saddle-appreciation time,' he replied, not altogether in jest.

Another friend of mine went wild and bought an enormously expensive Hermès saddle which sits on its own rack in front of the fireplace in her living-room. When I suggested that perhaps she could have spent the same amount of money on a horse of her own, she told me that in fact she didn't have nearly enough time to ride nor enough money to keep the horse at livery close to home. 'In four months I'd have turned over more money to that stable than I invested in this saddle,' she told me, 'and I'll have this forever.'

If you can't afford a saddle, don't buy a bridle instead but invest in a pair of stirrup leathers and irons as a less expensive alternative. A pair of stirrups in which your feet feel comfortable and secure can be a reassuring presence even on an unfamiliar horse or saddle, and you'll have the added advantage of not having to change the length each time you ride. Bridles are usually more difficult to fit to a particular horse, especially if he has been trained in a particular way or needs a special bit. Used saddles are not as expensive as new ones, and if you find one that fits you, go ahead and splurge. I got my jumping saddle that way, though my other saddle came into my possession just as both of my dogs and two of my cats did – from someone (in this case my aunt) who wanted me to give her old one a good home.

But when you do get yourself some tack, don't assume that you can walk into any old stable and use it. Be sure that the stable management approves and that the saddle fits the horse you are going to ride. If those technicalities can be ironed out, I guarantee that your enjoyment will be multiplied endlessly.

Other riders will be complimentary (as well as envious) and your self-confidence will grow with every ride.

Improving Your Chances to Ride

Another form of improving your morale is to expand your riding opportunities. In other words, learn to think like a horseless rider and don't be shy about it. I have mentioned elsewhere various methods of getting yourself a free ride or two – offering to exercise a friend's horse, mucking out a stable for a horse owner and so on. But there are other ways in which you can work horses into your life without revamping your lifestyle completely as you'd have to do if you owned a horse. This involves getting to know horse people, but not necessarily as a forlorn beggar in search of a horse.

The first step is to work out what you know that the horse owners around you do not. If you are interested in photography, for instance, get yourself and your camera around to local horse shows and take some pictures. Take notes on the names of your subjects (horses and riders) and if the pictures come out, send a print to the owner of the horse. Don't ask for money but offer your services as a photographer at the next show or inquire whether the owner might be interested in a portrait. Horse photography requires practice, and professionals are respected and plentiful in horsy areas, but if you have a gift and are willing to perfect it, you could find yourself combining your two interests to some advantage.

A good friend of mine (the illustrator for this book, incidentally) began his career as a commercial artist, drawing automobile tyres and aerosol cans for anyone who needed an attractive advertisement, but he always drew horses in his spare time just for the fun of it. One day he realized that his horses weren't half bad, and on the basis of some photographs taken at a horse race, he started to do some paintings of various prominent animals. Before long, thanks to the fact that his talent was made obvious in a couple of advertisements well placed in horse magazines, to say nothing of a couple of magazine covers and a gallery show held at horse-show time, he soon found himself the recipient of portrait commissions and now has built up for himself a nice business doing what he used to do just for fun.

As a book editor, I have found myself able at times to edit and publish books by experts in the horse field, as a result of which I have met some enormously interesting people who were willing to swap riding lessons for lessons in writing. Freelance writers with a special interest in horses can also turn their careers in an equestrian direction, by covering horsy events for newspapers or magazines, by doing books of their own, often in collaboration with horse people who don't write, and by working as consultants to equestrian organizations that need assistance in writing newsletters, press releases and other kinds of copy.

Accountants who ride can make themselves invaluable to stables that have erratic accounting or billing procedures or that need help at tax time. People who like to sew can help out horse people by lending (or trading for a ride) their expertise in making custom-made riding clothes. People in public relations can help stables to improve their image, enlarge their clientele or attract the public to their horse shows. Wizards in the insurance and banking fields can give financial advice, and lawyers can lend a legal hand – wearing two hats (hard and professional) to the local stables in times of need.

My husband is a veterinary surgeon, though not a horse specialist, but he does see the occasional horse and, of course, I trail along behind him carrying his bag, preparing syringes, comforting patients and otherwise making myself useful. Anyone with an equal love for animals and the medical profession has undoubtedly considered veterinary work, though it is a highly competitive field. A former assistant of my husband spent a year as a veterinary assistant in order to improve her chances of being accepted at a veterinary college. She found herself working for an equine practitioner who let her work in his 'recovery' barn full of horses in need of rest and rehabilitation, which meant tender loving care and regular exercise. And that, of course, meant regular riding for her, occasionally on some very fine animals.

Obviously you can't turn every sort of career into something that will make your presence at a stable necessary or useful, but it's worth thinking about in your spare time.

7
Hanging Around the Stable

One of the facets of horsemanship most ignored by horseless riders is that vast area known as stable or horse management, yet it is considered by all horsemen to be as important if not more so than the ability to win blue ribbons. As blue-ribbon winner Ian Millar of the Canadian Equestrian Team puts it: 'You must know when something is bothering the horse so you can reassure him. It's a matter of feel and the only way you can get that feel is to be with the horse, clean out his stall, be with him when he's happy, be with him when he's tired, and know him inside out.'

The only way to know a horse inside out, of course, is to know what he eats, when he eats it, when he sleeps and what his habits are, whether he has any special medical problems and how they are prevented or treated, and how to care for and clean him, his tack and his stall. All of that is what is meant by stable management, and all of that is what any horseless horseman must learn. If you like horses, learning won't be a drudge, though the work is sometimes hard and inconvenient. But it's also a way of earning free rides, so think of it as a carrot rather than a stick.

As I suggested earlier, the best way to learn about how a stable runs is to hang around before and after you ride. If your hour in the saddle starts at 10a.m., arrive at the stable at 9 or 9.30 and watch the horses being groomed and tacked up. When your ride is over, your horse may be handed over to the next rider or he may need to be taken back to the stable and cooled off or untacked or both. Someone has to do these things, and if the stable management allows, offer to be that someone. Learn by watching the grooms muck out the stalls or handle the horses, and ask questions so long as you don't run the risk of interfering with their work or otherwise making a pest of yourself.

Many public stables, camps and clubs offer instruction in stable management as well as in riding, and I strongly recommend that you take a course or two to get yourself familiar with the terms and the techniques involved. Although it is much easier to learn how to plait a mane, lunge a horse or clean a hoof by watching someone else than by reading the instructions in a book, there are several good basic books around that will give you a head start on subjects such as feeding, caring for tack or veterinary care. Keep in mind, though, that each horseman has his or her own methods, brand-name products and attitudes, so don't come on overconfident as a result of your book learning. Although there are many different titles available, three especially good ones are W. S. Codrington's *Know Your Horse* (J. A. Allen), A. Fraser and F. Manolson's *The Complete Book of Horse Care* (Pitman) and G. Wheatley's *Stable Management for the Owner Groom* (Cassell). All of these are geared to horse owners, but keep your mind open in any case. You might also like to get a reference copy of *Veterinary Notes for Horse Owners* by Horace M. Hayes (16th edition, Stanley Paul) and of *The Horse's Health from A to Z* by Peter Rossdale and Susan Wreford (David & Charles).

If you should be given a chance to work in a stable – either for money or free rides – don't hesitate to jump at the chance, for this is the best of all possible ways to learn. As Norman dello Joio says: 'Don't be afraid of work and don't be afraid to get your hands dirty.' He worked in stables as a groom for some years waiting for the chance to be an exercise rider and eventually a competitor, and feels that the experience was invaluable in preparing him for his career as an American Equestrian Team show jumper. If you feel that the person for whom you work is doing something wrong or something different from what you have read or learned elsewhere, don't argue or simply do things your own way but ask questions in the most tactful way. You may learn something new and (if you happen to be right) so may your boss. Until you know your way around, however, keep quiet as much as possible and do as you are instructed. These jobs are not easy to get, since many professionals feel that teaching someone the ropes takes more time and trouble than it's worth, and there are probably half a dozen people waiting right behind you for your job.

The following sections are not intended as a complete guide to the art of management, but cover various areas in which the horseless rider can learn enough to become valuable in assisting an owner either as an employee or as a volunteer. If you become experienced and proficient at these tasks, you may even find yourself in demand for jobs or at the very least invaluable to those people whose horses you want to ride.

Mucking Out

We might as well start with the least attractive and dirtiest part of the job, for this is the chore that nearly any owner would be delighted to turn over to someone else. Horses that are confined to boxes for all or part of the day when they are not being worked invariably soil the bedding, which must be kept clean if the animal isn't to develop ailments such as thrush, infections or respiratory disorders. A horse that is out in the pasture all day and kept in the box only at night will not do as much damage as a continuously stabled animal, but there will always be something to clean up. (And the pasture, too, must be kept clean, since intestinal parasites breed in manure and can reinfest a horse if the droppings are not removed.) One horse I know spends a good deal of time outside but always, without fail, urinates in his box the moment he is put in. He makes up for this by defecating always in the same part of his box, leaving the area around his feed bin pristine, but his stablemate makes up for *that* by carefully depositing his droppings in every possible corner of the box next door. My horse-loving aunt tells me that she once made a valiant effort to housebreak her mare by training her always to defecate in one part of the pasture on a pile of straw, but it never really worked, mainly because horses have little control over their bowel movements. They do control their urinating, however, since they are forced to take a special stance, and many horses will not urinate under saddle.

Equine habits aside, the problem with every horse is treated in the same way: mucking out. On a daily basis, droppings and wet bedding must be removed (usually with a pitch-fork or manure fork) and carted away (usually in a wheelbarrow) to the muck heap, which is generally near the stable, though not so near that flies and other manure lovers will be attracted into the stable itself. (This pile will be made smaller periodically either by someone's trucking it away or by removal to a compost heap where it can season before it is ready to use on the garden.) Don't make the mistake of removing more bedding than you need to, since it is expensive and perfectly reusable if not soiled.

Once a week – or more if necessary – the box should be given a thorough cleaning. Take the horse out of the box first, then remove the obvious manure and wet bedding. Then work your way around the box, picking up all the bedding, shaking it on the pitchfork to separate the soiled from the clean portion and set the clean stuff to one side. When you have dug down to the bottom all the way around, scrape it with a shovel and disinfect with lime, and then return the clean bedding to make a level layer, adding new bedding as necessary.

One thing to keep in mind as you muck out is the condition of the horse's manure. If there are many visible grains of feed in it, the horse is obviously not digesting his food, which may indicate tooth problems that should be brought to the attention of the owner. If the droppings are loose, discoloured or otherwise different from the normal quality and consistency, or if the urine is unusually coloured, tell someone about it. Keep an eye on the salt block, too. Most horses get mineral supplements and if the block is being used more rapidly than normal, there may be something the matter with the animal.

During this weekly session, it may also be necessary to wash the water and feed buckets or bins thoroughly with warm water and detergent (rinsing carefully), and to scrub down doors, windows, walls or whatever else seems in need of cleaning.

Whether you are doing the daily or the weekly chores, remember always to leave the centre aisle or the area outside the box as clean as possible. Nothing is untidier than a stable with loose wisps of hay or straw lying about, and nothing is more dangerous than leaving a wheelbarrow or a pitchfork around on the floor for human or horse to knock over or step onto.

Feeding and Watering

Most people who know their horses take great care in their choice of feed, method of feeding and schedule, since nutrition is such an important part of general equine health and condition. If you are given specific instructions about feeding a horse, follow them to the letter; if you are given no instructions, ask before you make some bad guesses. Horses that get a great deal of fresh grass in the pasture may get less food in the box than those who are confined; on the other hand, confined horses that are not worked hard may be fed less to keep them from getting more energy than they need, though they might have as much hay as they will eat to keep them occupied and contented. In other words, each horse has a different diet because nutritional requirements vary from one animal to the next. Some are worked harder than others; some are 'easy keepers' that need little food to keep them fit; some have deficiencies or medical problems that may require supplements or special feeds. The same horse may get a different diet at different times of the year, depending on weather, work and type of feed.

There are, however, a few useful generalizations about feeding horses that will help you get started. In preparing hay for a horse, don't simply throw a bale or part of one (called a 'flake') into the box. Outside the box, preferably in an area where the hay is stored, pull off the amount you will need and break it apart with your hands. Then lift a bit with a pitchfork and shake it to remove dust and to separate the stalks. Dust can be damaging to a horse's eyes or respiratory tract, and bits of twigs and rough stalks that fall out in the winnowing process can be rough on a horse's throat. If the hay still seems dusty, sprinkle some water on it. When you have a nice, light pile, convey it by fork to the horse's box – putting it on the floor near the bin (always in the same place – horses are creatures of habit, remember) unless there is an overhead hay rack.

In feeding grain, be sure that you measure properly using a special measuring can. Even if the horse has a feed bin built into the box, use a bucket to carry the grain to the bin and be sure to mix the grains together if you are using more than one type. Supplements or medications are often mixed into the grain, and you may be asked – if the horse tends to refuse 'tampered' feed – to lace the mixture with a few tablespoons of molasses to mask the taste. If you are feeding treats into the grain such as carrots or apples, don't break them into too small chunks that might be swallowed without chewing.

If you are given a regular schedule to follow, stick to it, and if you aren't, try to find out somehow at what times the horse is accustomed to eating. I have known perfectly placid animals raise perfect hell when their meals weren't delivered on time, and some have even reached such a state that their digestion was upset. The digestive tract of a horse is one of the most delicate things there is, and it seems that anything can disturb it, even tension or anxiety. So when you feed a horse, notice whether he is really eating or simply picking at the food. A horse that goes off his feed is giving a signal that something is wrong, and the sooner you know that the better your chances will be to prevent serious trouble. One way of stopping trouble before it starts is to make sure that the food you give is of the highest possible quality; if the hay and grain seem mouldy and the carrots and grass are less than fresh, complain to the owner, who is probably counting on you for that sort of information.

One substance that all horses get, regardless of individual diet, is water, and a normal horse will drink from eight to ten gallons a day. Stables that don't have watering devices have to have people willing to haul water buckets, i.e., people like you. Horses should have access to water most of the time, but there are exceptions to that rule. When a horse is hot from exertion or has been deprived of water for some time, it should be offered in very small quantities if at all; preferably, the horse should be cooled down before being allowed free access to the water bucket. It is easy to lead a horse to water but impossible to keep him from drinking if the bucket contains more water than you want him to have. So wait for a while before watering or don't fill the bucket to the top. And don't let water sit in a bucket for so long that it gets soiled or murky-looking, and be sure to break the ice from the top of a bucket in cold weather.

Grooming

Although show horses always seem to have been shined like well-polished silver, the point of grooming is not simply to keep a horse looking good. Horses that are stabled year-round need daily grooming to tone their muscles and to stimulate blood circulation and the glands that secrete the oils that keep the skin and coat soft and glossy. These horses may also be clipped during cold weather to keep their heavy winter coats under control, since the presence of a long hair coat will cause profuse sweating if a horse is heavily worked and this can lead to problems. Clipped horses must be blanketed if they are to be protected against the cold (sweat rugs are also used in warm weather to keep a horse from cooling off too fast). Horses that are pastured for most of the year will need only occasional brushing to remove clumps of dirt, mats, burrs, lice and so on to prevent skin trouble, but they should not be over-groomed, since they need a natural layer of oil and dust in the coat as a protective covering against the elements. (These horses should also not be overworked when their winter coats are heavy.)

Most grooms develop their own techniques and methods of grooming their charges, and the best way to learn is to apprentice yourself to someone who knows what he or she is doing. I won't go into the various chores here, but I can recommend that you become familiar with the tools of the trade and their uses: the currycomb, the body brush, the dandy or mud brush, the finishing brush, the rub rag or stable rubber, the sponge and the sweat scraper (used to give a horse a bath), the hoof pick, the mane comb and the clippers (usually electric or battery operated).

While you are watching your mentor at work on a horse, make yourself useful by keeping the tools clean (use the currycomb to clean the brushes, for instance) or by picking up clumps of dirt and hair that fall. Especially important to learn is the use of the hoof pick, since this is an object that you should carry with you on long rides in case the horse picks up a stone in his shoe. If you find yourself confronting a horse that you are

Many horses enjoy a cooling bath after a day's work

about to ride but must groom and tack up yourself, keep in mind that you should: (1) not go below the knees or onto any tender area with the currycomb, if you must use it at all (which is never on clipped or fine-skinned horses); (2) always brush in the direction in which the hair lies; (3) clean out the horse's feet; and (4) make sure that there is no dust or other foreign substance beneath the areas on which you put the tack. That's not much of a grooming job, but it is the essential minimum that you must do before riding.

Another reason to learn the grooming procedure properly is to become familiar with signs of ill health or injury that may require attention either from the owner or from the veterinary surgeon. Eyes, nose or ears that are runny or filled with mucus, teeth that are broken or malformed, sores or cuts on the skin, areas that are sensitive to the touch, or hot areas on the legs and feet may all indicate trouble — some more serious than others. Loss of hair or a particularly dry coat or rigid skin can indicate anything from nutritional deficiency to parasites (worms) or even serious disease, and it is always the groom who notices these things first. Read up on horse health and be sure to be on hand when the vet turns up for his regular visit or in an emergency. Many vets got their start by taking an interest in equine health, and some of them are horsemen still.

Clipping and plaiting are two jobs that are time consuming but demanding in terms of skill and are often up for grabs if there is someone around willing to undertake them. These procedures are usually reserved for horses that are shown, hunted or raced regularly and are useful to know if you plan to go into competition yourself, but any horse that is stabled or used frequently during the cold weather will probably need clipping even if plaits never grace his neck. Not only is a clipped horse more attractive and easier to clean; he is also easier to cool down, since the sweat evaporates more quickly to keep the animal's internal temperature level. Most horses need clipping only twice a year (late October and January), but draft horses, Shetland ponies and other animals with fast-growing haircoats will need to be clipped more often. Clipping should not be done toward the end of winter as the new haircoat is beginning to grow in; at this time of year, the shedding process will have begun and the groom will be busy just grooming!

There are different types of clips, one of them involving the whole horse, one (the hunter clip) leaving the legs and saddle area unclipped, and one (the trace clip) leaving all but the lower part of the shoulder, belly and hindquarters fully furred. But learning the pattern is only the first step. Next you must learn to wield the clippers in such a way that the hair is removed evenly and neatly from such hard-to-reach areas as around the ears, the dock (tail area) and the legs. Some horses don't care much for the sound though they will get used to it in time; one friend of mine owns a horse that objects so violently to the noise of large clippers that he has to tranquilize the animal and then use a pair of small clippers, which take a long time to cover very little area. If the job begins to get you down, just remember that your grooming chores will be a lot easier after clipping and be grateful that you weren't a groom in the good, old days when clipping was done by hand with a razor or with a candle to singe the long hairs.

Plaiting is the ultimate procedure in mane care, used for show, hunting and for training the mane to lie flat. There are many traditions, rules and techniques for plaiting, and here again, learning is best done by watching or by working under the eagle eye of an expert. Tails may also be plaited, either for show or for practicality on muddy days. There are many other things to do with these parts of the horse in addition to keeping them combed and clean: pulling or plucking involves pulling a few hairs at a time along the edge of the upper tail to keep it neat and pulling the long hairs from the mane to keep it between four and six inches long; banging involves cutting the long hair of the tail straight across the bottom even with the hock; hogging involves clipping the mane flat to the neck; and roaching is clipping the mane but leaving the centre hairs slightly longer. Some horses, such as Arabs, wear a bridle-path style mane, which means that the mane is hogged for about a third of the way down the neck from behind the ears to show off the animal's neck and to make the bridle easier to put on. Some cuts are chosen because of tradition or breed, while others are selected because they show the horse to advantage, masking faults or highlighting strong points. If you are going to play hairdresser to someone else's horse, be sure that you clear the style selection with them, but if you show some talent, you may find yourself the Vidal Sassoon of the stable.

Tack

Anyone who has gone beyond the beginner stage in riding should know how to put on a bridle and saddle and how to take them off, but it never ceases to amaze me how many horseless riders – even those with a good deal of skill in the saddle – seem to believe that horses were born with tack in place. Because their animals have been led out to them fully tacked and are led away tacked after the ride, they have never had the chance to learn either procedure. But what should happen if they find themselves confronted with a naked horse? Refuse to ride? Put things on backwards? Horrible thoughts to contemplate. Any skier or fisherman worth his salt knows his equipment inside and out, and it stands to reason that anyone who plans to ride more than once should know not only how to work his equipment, but how it is made, cared for and repaired.

As plastic takes over the world, I find that one of the aspects of riding that gives me special pleasure is the fact that there is so much lovely, smelly leather around. But leather requires good care if it is to stay in good condition and care means work – often a lot of it. Saddles and bridles and martingales and head collars and breastplates and stirrup leathers and girths and all those leather items need constant cleaning – brushing off of dust, dirt or dried sweat or saliva after each use, frequent applications of saddle soap and weekly (or more frequent) thorough cleaning, which involves taking the bridle and saddle apart, checking for signs of wear, and sponging or scrubbing, wiping dry, and oiling. Leather that is not cared for carefully will dry out, rot or break apart, and leather tack that is in poor condition will be uncomfortable and potentially dangerous for

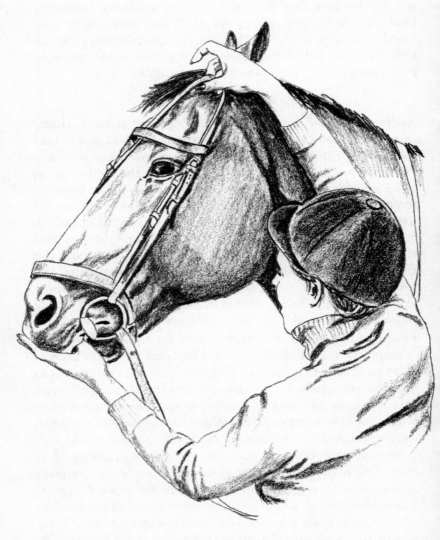

Even if you don't have your own horse, you should learn the proper way to put on a bridle (left) before a ride, and to untack a horse after a ride, replacing the bridle with a head collar (right)

both man and beast. The metal parts will also need an occasional thorough soaking and scrubbing with metal cleaner, and fabrics, as in the saddle pad or numnah and girth, will also need washing, drying and brushing.

The first step is to learn how the various items are put together, and that means taking them apart, cleaning them and putting them back in the proper way. Learning to put them on the horse is step two: usually done saddle first, martingale (if any) second and bridle last. Although many horses consent to being tacked up in their boxes, some prefer to be tacked up (and groomed) on cross-ties outside the stall. Whatever you do, don't let the horse loose until you are sure that everything is in place and you are in control; nothing is more embarrassing than having a half-tacked animal wandering around without its bridle on. Some horses object to being tacked up and have picked up a number of tricks to put first-timers or novices off their stride. 'Blowing up' or expanding the belly to make the girth difficult (or impossible) to tighten is one; if a sharp but not damaging blow to the belly doesn't convince the horse to breathe out, simply walk the animal around until he releases the air and tighten the girth then. Some horses cowkick when the girth is tightened, or flatten their ears in a threatening manner. Don't let yourself get into a vulnerable position relative to the legs and keep up a constant chatter and a confident manner so that the horse will be reassured and know you mean business. I once knew a mare who was so head shy that the bridle had to be taken almost entirely apart before she would allow it to be put on; I assumed that she had ear problems, since she seemed so sensitive, but I found that she was perfectly content to let me remove the bridle no matter how firmly I pressed on her ears in the process. I didn't alert the vet but thought she could be worked out of this bad habit with some painstaking care. (It turned out that the groom had already taken such care, but the mare was unusually stubborn so we just continued to take the bridle apart each time.)

Removing tack is much easier than putting it on, but here you must take care to leave it in the proper way – clean and suitably stored to avoid damage to the structure or the materials. Most horses in large stables have their own tack and the places for it should be carefully marked with the animals' names; if you are confused, ask. An error here can be a great deal of discomfort for the horse or confusion for the next rider.

You'll notice that I haven't described the proper procedures for tacking up and down and that's because it would take many pages to do so when one watching session will do. There are different methods, but the one that works is obviously the best, so if you find yourself having trouble dressing a particular horse, adapt what you know to what he seems willing to tolerate, so long as you don't let him take advantage of you. It should go without saying that most of your tacking-up procedures should be carried out on the near (left) side of the horse, the one from which most people mount and dismount; you will, of course, need to visit the other side occasionally to tighten the girth and pull the stirrups up and down.

Exercising and Hot-walking

Obviously the horseless rider's chief aim in hanging around a stable is to be allowed to exercise the inhabitants, but riding isn't the only way this is done. For one thing, you must learn how to lead a horse properly which, surprisingly enough, is not as simple as it seems. A bridled horse should be led only for short distances by the reins; for anything longer than that one must remove the bridle, replace it with a halter (or put a halter on over the bridle) and use a lead shank. If the horse you are leading by the reins is skittish or seems anxious to get away from you, do not bring the reins over his head (he could step on a rein if he gets away from you) but hold the reins rather closely beneath his jaw for firm control. If the horse is tired or placid or well-behaved, pull the reins over the head and, holding the horse just under the jaw with your right hand, place the rest of the reins in your left so that they don't get stepped on. Also, be sure that you pull the stirrups up on the saddle so that they don't flap around on the horse's sides. Even if you are using a headcollar and lead shank, don't get careless and allow the lead

Walking hot horses or cooling off young racehorses in training is one of the various jobs available at the race track and large stables

to get too slack; I've had more than one halter ring break on me because a grazing horse managed to step firmly on the lead and pull his head up suddenly.

I have discussed elsewhere the methods of lungeing and long-reining, two ways of giving a horse exercise without getting aboard, especially useful in schooling or when you haven't enough time to ride. Stables large and opulent enough to afford an automatic walker can take care of this task for you, but the horse will need constant supervision and you should know how it works, in case of emergency or misfire. These walkers are used for cooling down as well as for exercise, and this is a technique that any stablehand must learn to perfection if only because overheating can cause so many problems. If a horse comes back from a ride sweating and hot, curse the rider who brought him back that way and plan to spend fifteen or twenty minutes cooling the horse off. Leading the horse around and allowing him to graze is the most natural way, but you may also have to put on a sweat rug (to avoid chilling) and keep the horse away from the watering trough. You may also have to give the animal a bath and scrape off the water and sweat, and then walk around until the horse is completely dry. Don't ever put any horse back in a box when it is still hot, and don't let it drink much water until its temperature and respiration have returned to normal.

Hot-walking is a job unto itself around the race track, where the horses are delicate, young and prone to high-spirits. Many young people get into the business of exercise riding and eventually jockeying or training that way, so it needn't be pointed out that this is a useful thing to know how to do.

If a horse is to be turned out to the paddock or pasture for exercise, relaxation or for a period of time, be sure that you know exactly where to put the horse and what other animals are in there. Some horses will fight if pastured together, and more than several of them have got out by poorly fastened gates or fences that have fallen into disrepair. If you have any questions, don't guess but ask. And don't let the horse go until you are well within the paddock with the gate closed behind you. It's easier for you to reopen it to get out or climb over the fence than it is to chase an animal who has the whole world to explore.

8
Broadening Your Horizons

Up to this point we've been doing a lot of learning, what with instructors, lessons, sessions in the school and on the bridle path, and experience on as many horses as possible. Although horsemen never stop learning, there comes a time in every rider's life when the basics become second nature and the real challenge lies in being able to prove to yourself and to others that you *can* ride and that you can do it well. For some people, it is enough simply to be able to enjoy a cross-country hack for its own sake or to be satisfied with that hard-earned ability to ride whatever horse comes along. But to many other people, the proving ground is a show ring, a race track, a polo field or a piece of the countryside in which foxes abide. After all, riding is a sport and, as in other sports, the name of the game is competition. Whether you compete for prizes or fun, for the thrill of winning or for the satisfaction of holding your own in the company of like-minded sportsmen, this is what it's all about. Some of the activities described in this chapter will mean a change of scene, dress or equipment, others, only a change of attitude, many will demand special training of the horse as well as the rider. But none of them demands that you own a horse, and most of them take place year-round throughout the country.

Horse Shows

If the stable at which you ride puts on a regular horse show or a series of them, your instructor or the stable manager will probably encourage you to enter one as you make progress with your riding. Even a fairly advanced show geared to top riders and horses will generally have one or more classes for less experienced riders and for the horseless variety who must rely on the stable's own animals. If the stable does not sponsor any shows, and if there are none in your area, suggest that the management put one on or offer to do so for them. There is a lot of work involved in managing a horse show, even a small, informal one, but there is a great deal of satisfaction as well, especially if the atmosphere is properly competitive – not dog-eat-dog but active and spirited. All you really need is a head for organization, a set of rosettes (available through saddlery shops), and, of course, some interested people to enter the various classes. If your stable's management hasn't had any experience, write to the British Horse Society for information about rules and read L. C. Cooper's *Horse Show Organisation* (J. A. Allen). The main point is to get everyone into the act – plaiting manes, grooming horses within an inch of their dapples (or closer, if you want them to shine), setting up jumps or musical stalls, as well as the less horsy chores, such as announcing, selling refreshments, collecting entry fees, handing out numbers and presenting rosettes to the winners. The function of a stable or schooling show is for everyone to get experience and to have fun, not just to win prizes. Judges should be expert horsemen (not the stable's own instructors but perhaps instructors from other stables), and they should be encouraged to help out all entrants, winners and losers, by giving constructive criticism when asked and by awarding as many rosettes as there are colours in the rainbow.

First prize – blue	Sixth prize – green
Second prize – red	Seventh prize – purple
Third prize – yellow	Eighth prize – brown
Fourth prize – white	Ninth prize – gray
Fifth prize – pink	Tenth prize – light blue

Grand champion – blue, red, yellow and white
Reserve to grand champion – red, yellow, white and pink
Champion – blue, red and yellow
Reserve champion – red, yellow and white

Larger shows are usually affiliated to the British Horse Society or the British Show Jumping Association and, like the informal, unaffiliated shows, are divided into jumping and showing classes. Although equitation classes (where the rider rather than the horse's performance is judged) are occasionally offered, most classes involve horses being shown in hand (led by the handler) or under saddle, both on the flat and, in hunter classes, over a small course of jumps as well. Classes will vary considerably according to the level of competition, but except for breed and conformation classes, the emphasis is on performance rather than appearance, and this is where the rider's skill is as important as the horse's natural ability or degree of schooling. All horses entered in affiliated shows must be registered with the BHS or the BSJA, and are put into classes (C, B and A), according to the amount of prize money they have won. (Severe penalties may be incurred by exhibitors who knowingly put a horse of a higher grade into a lower grade class.)

In addition to riding classes, there is also a harness division in which hackney ponies are shown for style and pace; private driving classes usually involve wheeling through an obstacle course. There is even a three-day event (often held in one day, however) for driving horses, involving a dressage phase, a cross-country run and an obstacle test in which time is a crucial factor.

Entering a horse show need not be a difficult matter. A few days before the show, study the prize list to determine which classes will be suitable for your level of expertise (and your horse's level, if you are entering an affiliated show). Fill out an entry blank for each class and make sure that your instructor will be on hand to coach you (there may be an additional fee for that). If you are going to be sharing a horse with another horseless rider, be sure that there are no conflicts in your selection of classes and that the poor animal doesn't get overworked by entering too many. Other than that, your only worry will be to get yourself properly turned out. On the day of the show, make sure that the horse is groomed and tacked up (and his mane plaited, if necessary) and that you are registered and have received your number. Be ready at the collecting ring several minutes before your class begins, boots polished, number in place and nerves at ease. There may be some time for you to school the horse a bit, not do do any last-minute cramming as for an examination but to do some trotting about to relax yourself and the horse. When your class is called, walk serenely into the ring and do your stuff – and don't forget to smile. In some classes, the horses and riders perform individually and you must wait your turn; don't use those few minutes to sit there and fret but watch the competition if you can or think pleasant thoughts.

There is no avoiding the fact that you will need a good horse or pony to do well at the better shows against strong competition from people with their own mounts, but even here the horseless rider has a chance. Ask someone who owns a horse but isn't interested in showing whether you might borrow the animal for a particular event (and preferably for a period before the show so that you may practise). If you should do well, the owner will be as pleased as you are and may encourage you to ride the horse at other shows. Several famous riders got their start doing just this kind of thing – called 'catch riding' – for fun and ribbons at first and eventually for money or for the chance to go on the horse-show circuit or even onto the Equestrian Team. Just as dog shows have their professional handlers, so horse shows have their professional riders. The next time you go to a show, notice in the programme how many horses don't belong to the people who are riding them. Harvey Smith is probably the most renowned rider in the show jumping field, just as Steve Cauthen has become a superstar as a race rider; neither one of them reached the top of their professions riding their own animals! (In the next chapter we will look further into the world of the professional rider.)

Because many excellent riders do not have the time or money to support their own stables full of competition horses, they tend to rely on the generosity of sponsors or employees – well-to-do individuals with a great interest in horses and with trophy rooms waiting for rosettes but without the children or ability to ride the horses they own. If you are fortunate and talented enough to attract the attention of one of these people, count your blessings. But even if you are not, you can work at a somewhat less glamorous level by making your presence known to horse owners as someone who could do well by their horses simply for the privilege of keeping the rosettes rather than for any money or other support. (Some excellent young riders with an eye on the Olympics are concerned about keeping their amateur status and do not accept money or jobs as professionals, though they may accept gifts and expenses, such as riding clothes or paid-for trips to shows.) Catch riders have some responsibilities as well as pleasures, however, which include undertaking the risk of injury (unless there is written

Rodney Jenkins, the top professional show jumper in the United States, has reached that exalted height on the backs of many other people's horses

agreement, though most horse owners will usually cover the cost of medical bills), the purchase and maintenance of an appropriate and impeccable wardrobe, the keeping of accurate records, and the responsibility for being on time for each class – to say nothing of riding each horse as if it were one's own.

Devoting a great deal of time to the horse-show circuit can be a big commitment, and as the business of showing becomes more popular and the horses become more expensive, the costs can be considerable as well. But Ian Millar, a member of the Canadian Equestrian Team, has some reassuring words for the horseless:

> There is an old hang-up about this sport. In certain levels of horse showing, rich people get involved and buy their kids nice horses and they win. But in show jumping, all the money in the world won't help you. You've got to know how to ride a horse. And so my advice to young people is not to get discouraged if they don't have money. All the industry, owners, trainers, and the like are always looking for a young rider with talent. I can't think of a rider or trainer who won't bend over backward to help that talented person. The horse shows are full of young people who are working as grooms now. If they show their aptitude, they'll be allowed to ride and to jump a little bit. So it is possible to ride and get to the Grand Prix level without having a million dollars.

Gymkhanas

Games on horseback come in all shapes, sizes and degree of seriousness. A Hindu word for 'field day', the gymkhana was invented by British cavalrymen stationed in India, but the event has now become popular throughout the world, mostly as a sport for youngsters. No special tack is required as long as it is comfortable for the horse, and riding apparel for the rider will depend on the rules of the show, which may be part of a large horse show, a spontaneous, informal backyard event or a more formal occasion.

Informal gymkhanas can be as simple or as complex as the imagination of the participants and instigators of the show, but they usually include races against the clock, competitive games and non-competitive games. Speed races can be anything from ring spearing (as in jousting matches of old), racing from a starting point around a pole and back, Coke or beer races (in which riders must ride to a barrel, drink a full can of liquid, turn it upside down without spilling any, and ride back across the finish line), to Gambler's Choice, in which riders try to jump a series of jumps each worth a number of points according to difficulty, and accumulate the largest number of points in the shortest time. Competitive games include musical stalls or tyres (run like musical chairs), egg-and-spoon races, relay races, backing races, and the one pound-note marathon (a bareback class in which a pound note is placed under each rider's seat – the winner being the rider who keeps the pound note the longest through the walk, trot and canter). Non-competitive games, such as tag, Simon says and follow the leader, are particularly good for very young children, since the rules are the same as those played on foot.

With a good basic seat and experience on many different horses, a young rider may look forward to a successful future in the show ring

My particular favourite is one whose outcome is invariably up to the horse: bobbing for apples, in which horses and riders race to one end of a ring where riders dismount and try to get their animals to bob for apples in buckets of water. Not until a horse has picked up an apple can the rider remount and race back across the finish line. Everyone knows that you can lead a horse to water and not make him drink, but the sight of ten youngsters trying to defy the old adage is worth is weight in Polaroids.

For some ideas about the kinds of games that may be included in a gymkhana, take a look at *Mounted Games and Gymkhanas*, published by the British Horse Society.

Dressage Tests

We have already considered dressage in the chapter on instruction as a style of riding and a method of training, but it is becoming increasingly popular as a competitive sport in itself as well as a famous spectacle performed by the 'high school' horses of the Spanish Riding School in Vienna, the Cadre Noir of Saumur, in France, and the Andalusian Riding School in Spain. Andalusians, Arabs and Lippizaners perform exhibitions of 'airs above the ground', but competitive dressage, like the system itself, begins with elementary levels and progresses to increasingly higher levels, culminating with the Olympic Games.

A dressage test is held in a special arena, marked with letters at the corners and along the sides, and each horse and rider perform a prescribed series or pattern of movements one at a time while one or more judges comment and keep score. There are usually two or three tests for each level, starting with the Training Level, Test 1, and working up through First, Second, Third and Fourth levels, to Prix St-Georges, Reprise, Intermédiaire and the Grand Prix de Dressage which is an Olympic test. The tests are increasingly difficult, of course, and the standards by which the horses are judged become higher as the level rises. In other words, less will be expected of a trot at the Training Level than at a higher level.

Before you decide that dressage is out of your league because you don't have a horse you can work with on a daily basis, ask your teacher for some dressage instruction or apply to a special dressage instructor and work, even on an intermittent basis, with a horse to which you do have access. Keep in mind that the first test of the Training Level involves only being able to walk, trot and canter on correct leads going both ways around the school, making smooth transitions from one gait to the next (halt and walk, walk and trot, trot and canter) and making smooth circles while changing direction. Of course, those gaits must be sufficiently balanced and rhythmic to win points, but this is what every rider wants from every horse he rides. More advanced tests include collection and extension, complicated patterns and various lateral or two-track movements (such as the shoulder-in) as well as turns on the haunches and ten-metre cantered circles.

For information regarding dressage tests and clubs in your area, write to the Dressage Committee of the British Horse Society.

Long-distance Riding

Trail riding is often simply a pleasant way to see the countryside from horseback, but it is also an activity in which riders may compete at various levels – from light to severe, depending on the type of terrain and the required time in which it must be covered. This is a relatively new sport in Britain, but one that is rapidly gaining in popularity; there are about thirty competitive rides held each year, culminating in the Golden Horse Shoe Ride and the International 100 Mile Ride. These rides generally take place over two days and there are frequent veterinary checks along the way to ensure that the horses remain sound. The average pace for one of the top rides is about nine miles an hour, but points are deducted if the finishing horse is not in top condition.

Preparing for a long-distance ride can involve months of conditioning, therefore, as well as training in specifics such as backing, dealing with steep hills and difficult footing, and working on extended gaits, particularly the trot. Although most competitors ride their own horses – and some enthusiasts are trying to breed the best possible animals for distance riding – many riders have done well on other people's horses, hired or borrowed, so long as the horses are fit and properly prepared. There are few frills involved in this sport – no special apparel or tack, though what one wears or puts on one's horse must be perfectly fitted for the sake of comfort. It is not necessary to have any particular type of horse, either, except one that is capable of doing the job. Arabs or part-Arabs seem to do best in long-distance competition, although thoroughbreds and light, athletic animals also do well, unlike the heavier, stockier breeds.

The best way to break into this field is to get to know some people who participate in the sport and to offer to help them condition their horses, which consists of many long rides that are both demanding and time-consuming. The most valuable book I have found on the subject is Ann Hyland's *Endurance Riding* (American publisher Lippincott) which covers everything from horse-shoeing to feeding and training, but there is also a new booklet published by the Long-Distance Committee of the British Horse Society, from which source you may also be able to find out about long-distance rides throughout Britain.

Combined Training

There are three phases in this very popular equestrian sport: dressage, cross-country work and stadium jumping. I have already discussed the first and third of these phases (the latter as a part of horse shows), but the second phase is probably the most taxing of the three, as it involves a very demanding course or series of courses over obstacles of various descriptions ridden against the clock. Unlike steeplechasing or race riding over jumps, the cross-country phase of combined training is undertaken by one horse and rider at a time. Speed is what counts, although points are deducted for falls, refusals and running off course. Designing cross-country courses for horse trials is an art requiring imagination and general fiendishness, for the obstacles are not only imposing looking at high-level competitions but they are demanding in other ways, such as appearance (stacks of tyres, for instance, or picnic tables) and pure difficulty (complicated in-and-outs, two jumps separated by a steep hill, jumps in the middle of streams or ditches, and so on for five miles or more at high speed). A horse that is able to cope with such a course must be a talented jumper in top condition, but more than that he must be unusually brave and trusting in his rider.

A horse and rider team that can manoeuvre the cross-country phase after a dressage trial and before a relatively simple course of stadium jumping is a special combination indeed and this is why this particular sport is considered perhaps the ultimate in all-round competitive events. Whether the horse trial takes place in one day or three, when it is called three-day eventing and is one of the three equestrian sports in the Olympic Games, it is a demanding activity. An event horse

Cross-country jumping is a demanding but exhilarating way for the experienced horse and rider to enjoy working together

must be willing, athletic and perfectly conditioned, and so must the rider. There are several different levels of competition, beginning with the Pre-Training Level and culminating in the Olympics. For information about the time and location of horse trials during the year, write to the Horse Trials Committee of the British Horse Society. There are several excellent books on the subject, namely: *Eventing* by Caroline Silver (Collins), *Eventing in Focus* by Jeremy Beale, with wonderful illustrations by Alix Coleman (Angus & Robertson) and *The Event Horse* by Sheila Wilcox (Pelham Books).

Needless to say, because of the nature of each phase, combined training involves a great deal of work with a single horse, and if you don't own one, you must be able to have regular access to a prospect. Although Richard Meade, like other Equestrian Team members has done extremely well on borrowed horses, he has had to work with them for weeks if not months to arrive at performance condition. If you don't have such access, you can, of course, work at dressage, cross-country jumping and stadium jumping on different horses, perfecting your own skills so that when a good horse does come along, you'll be ready for him. In the meantime, go out and watch some trials; you'll learn a great deal just seeing the experts at work and you may find yourself in company with some like-minded enthusiasts who just might be willing to coach you or form a group with you under the instruction of an expert.

Fox-hunting

For many people the whole point of learning to ride is to become skilled enough to spend mornings during the autumn and winter chasing a fox over hill and dale and fence and wall, together with a pack of hounds and a full array of beautifully dressed riders to whom traditional etiquette and proper behaviour seem as important as equestrian skill. Actually, in spite of the various enemies that fox-hunters have gained over the years (angry farmers with trampled fields, humane souls who worry for the foxes and overused horses and earthy folks who think all the fuss is absurd), this activity can be one of the most exciting ways to spend time on horseback. In many areas where foxes are no longer abundant hares may be chased or vulpine scents 'dragged' to give the hounds something to chase, and the bloody aspect of the sport has diminished considerably. Hunters nowadays are far more conscientious about crossing private property without permission (it's not that easy to gallop through a housing development); they are also far more sensible in their use of horses. No longer will you see streams of thrill-crazy gents and side-saddled ladies landing with a thump on their horses' kidneys as they race headlong through the fields and over the walls leaning as far back as possible. The forward or hunt seat has become pretty universal and the pace is more reasonable these days, though the atmosphere is no less spirited. In fact, even if you haven't had much (or any) jumping experience, you can still join a hunt, since most obstacles have walk-arounds and some of them – the stone walls in particular – get lower as the hunt progresses, turning into veritable gravel by the time the last riders reach them.

Nevertheless, hunting is still quite a sport and not one for the poor or timid. Formal hunting has very specific rules of conduct and dress, so if you are asked to join a pack for a hunt, be sure to bone up on the rules and get yourself some appropriate riding apparel, which you can usually borrow or hire if this is going to be a one-time outing on your part. Be sure to read the British Horse Society booklet, *A Hunting Reminder* by Dorian Williams, before you go just to brush up on the rules of dress and conduct.

And prepare yourself for a good workout as well. If you are accustomed to a few laps around the ring at a canter, you'll find that a ten-minute cross-country gallop will take your breath away. A friend of mine went hunting for the first time aboard a hedgehog-coloured pony named Alvin. He had hoped for a few minutes to get to know the pony but the hounds 'found' at the first covert, whereupon the field was off and running. The run lasted for a good half hour after which our friend sought in vain for an oxygen mask in his sandwich case; he could have pulled up to catch his breath somewhere but that would have left him and his horse deserted in unfamiliar country. Although he found his second wind somewhere and continued (that was to be the only real run of the day), my friend suggests that first-time riders get themselves into condition before they put on their boots and breeches.

According to one instructor friend, a rider is ready to hunt when he or she can jump a three-foot fence in the ring, is comfortable on the cross-country gallop, can jump uphill and downhill fences as well as ditches and has had experience in large group trail rides. Alexander Mackay-Smith, a former Master of Fox Hounds, suggests that one rides an experienced horse alongside a 'pilot', an escort who knows the countryside and can keep an eye on you. He advises that the first-time hunter start off during the cubbing season, before the formal hunt season, when the young foxes are being encouraged to run cross-country. (The rules of dress are less formal then and the pace somewhat slower.) He also believes that novices should be warned not to interfere with the hunt staff or the hounds by chatting unnecessarily nor to interfere with the hounds by deviating from the path. If you have had enough and must go home, ask for the Master's permission and follow his directions. Stop if you hear hounds coming your way and if you do 'head' a fox (cause it to change direction) admit it. Don't hide behind a tree, even though you are embarrassed; point out the direction the fox took and you'll be able to show your face at the hunt breakfast later in the day.

The jumps that one usually encounters on a hunt are not easily knocked-down crossrails but solid fences, walls and banks (only the stone walls may diminish in size during the hunt), but don't worry too much that your horse will run out or stop, for most animals enjoy the chase as much as the riders and are eager to take whatever lies in their path. If anything, you should worry about your horse getting overexcited and racing ahead, since it is absolutely forbidden for anyone, member or guest, to overtake the Master of Fox Hounds, who leads the hunt. If you are new to the sport or even just new to this particular pack, play it safe and stay at the back of the field.

Although hunting has traditionally been a fairly exclusive

activity, many packs throughout the country do allow the public to join (consult *Bailey's Hunting Directory* for addresses), and most can provide horses for the occasion. Subscriptions can be high, though, so plan to spend several pounds for a day's outing, including horse and transportation. Although the horse may be unfamiliar to you, he will probably be familiar with the countryside, a great advantage to the first-timer. As Mr Mackay-Smith suggests, the best way to be introduced to the sport is to have someone along to show you the ropes — preferably a member of the hunt. If you don't feel that you are up to hunting on horseback, you can always watch the proceedings by following the hunt on foot or in a car. There are always others who will join you in this horseless activity and it can be fun, although I'll vow that you will be itching to ride before you reach the top of the first hill.

If you enjoy hunting but have a competitive urge and don't feel up to combined training, you might be interested in entering a hunter trial, a modified cross-country event over a mile or more of hunting country. They are no longer so popular or widespread as they once were, but Pony Clubs and some hunts still sponsor them.

Polo

This is another sport that was not designed for the timid or insecure rider. It has everything that football, ice hockey and rugby boast, and more — because it's all played on horseback. (Even the referee or official rides a horse.) And for the horsy set, polo is special because it demands the utmost in teamwork from its players, horses and humans alike. For years polo was a sport for the very rich. Players had their own strings of ponies because the game is demanding enough to require as many as three or four mounts for each match. But horseless riders have always been a part of polo, too, even in the Western United States where playing polo is an occasional byline of cowboys who double as players for their polo-enthusiastic employers. Although riding herd on cattle seems worlds apart from riding herd on a small white ball, the two activities do require much the same kind of skill. Polo ponies (which as often as not are thoroughbreds) are quick starters and short stoppers, able to turn on a sixpence and change leads at the drop of a heel. They must be alert to the action, and from what I've seen, the ponies are often quicker than their riders to spot the ball and chase after it. This kind of riding demands superb balance and instant reflexes from the rider, and the game itself demands teamwork from the players. Most important, however, is the teamwork between horse and rider, both of whom must share a love and understanding of the game and a fantastic disregard for personal safety.

These days, polo seems to be turning into a game for everyone, even women, now that men are finally willing to recognize female talents in the equestrian world (note the increased number of women in international jumping competitions or working as exercise riders and jockeys at race tracks). Although aggressiveness is an important characteristic of a good player, the ability to anticipate the play and a sense of timing are far more important than physical strength or even equestrian talent. In fact, the riding style is pretty unorthodox, since the rider is often well out of the saddle, the legs having little or no contact with the horse and the reins being held loosely in the left hand. But balance is essential as well as a complete understanding between horse and rider of the signals for stopping, turning and speeding up. Most experienced polo players will admit that at least seventy-five per cent of the game depends on the horse, and well-schooled polo ponies are very valuable for that reason. But you needn't own a string or even one pony to play. There are polo clubs throughout the country, and several centres sponsor polo teams. Ponies, together with the money to support them, are often donated by older players so that the costs aren't high for the horseless. Consult the Hurlingham Polo Association for information (204 Idol Lane, London EC3).

Gymnastics (or Vaulting)

This sport is growing in popularity – whether because of the horses involved or because the idea of being a Nadia Comaneci on horseback is so attractive, I really couldn't say. There is something of the circus-horse charm about gymnastics as well, since the riders do all sorts of athletic tricks as their animals revolve around the ring. Actually, this activity is far more demanding for rider than horse, although one needs a well-schooled, obedient animal willing to canter around in circles (often at the end of a lunge line) while someone performs movements on its back. One needn't be a superb rider to excel at the sport, but a good sense of balance and a certain amount of flexibility and skill are required. And the horse will need a special vaulting surcingle, a leather-padded girthlike affair with two handles to hold on to while doing vaults on and off, handstands, and the various other moves on and around the horse. Vaulting is an ancient branch of horsemanship going back to Roman times, and it is a highly competitive sport in Europe today especially among children. There are six basic compulsory exercises (the riding seat, the kneel and flag, the mill, the flank, the free stand and the scissors), and a competition team of eight members must perform all of these as well as a five-to-seven minute freestyle programme of combination exercises. Many coaches feel that this sport promotes self-confidence and skill in children who are learning to ride.

The two activities that follow are not competitive or highly organized like those we have been exploring. In fact, about all they have in common is that the saddles and hence the riding styles are different from those that the average horseless rider is likely to confront. But because the motto of the horseless rider is adaptability and because our *modus operandi* is to be ready to ride whatever is offered whenever, I thought it might be worth considering them as part of the broader horizon.

Sidesaddle

Until very recent years the sidesaddle has been regarded as a thing of the past, but recently we have seen something of a revival of this elegant, traditional and downright strange-looking method of riding a horse. Reserved for ladies for whom riding astride was considered most unladylike, this form of riding came into fashion during the eighteenth century and remained *de rigeur* in many parts of the world until well into the twentieth century. The sidesaddle made it possible for ladies to ride in full skirts without compromising their modesty, although it made riding a perilous business – especially in the hunting field – until the development in the mid-nineteenth century of the third pommel which helped to give the rider some measure of security. Horses had to be specially selected and trained to carry their sidesaddles and riders, for it was impossible to rise, to ride a two-point position at the gallop and over jumps, and to control both sides of the horse with leg pressure. Horses thus had to have steady, slow trots, strong shoulders to manage gallops and jumps without much help from the rider, and sensitive responses to the use of the leg on the near side (the left) and to the whip on the off, or right, side.

This form of riding is now enjoying a new surge of interest, and it is not surprising to see sidesaddle classes at horse shows or to see ladies riding to hounds quite unastride. Although poor sidesaddle horsemanship is hardly a joy to watch (or perform), seeing a fine horsewoman decked out in a special habit and sitting elegantly to the trot can be a real pleasure.

If you are ever offered the chance to ride sidesaddle, give it a try. The most important thing to remember is to keep your balance as centred as possible, without leaning at all (either forwards, backwards or sideways), sitting as straight as you can and remaining as relaxed as you can manage. If you have learned to ride a jog or sitting trot, you shouldn't have too much trouble maintaining both your position and your cool; the walk and the canter (providing you can get the horse to respond to the appropriate aid for the appropriate lead), should be a cinch. The idea is not to grip and clutch but to move in rhythm, with the motion of the horse rather than against it. Although I can't recommend jumping until you have attained some degree of confidence and security, chances are that you won't fall off if you remember that the horse is the one doing the work, not yourself. Don't interfere with him (which means keeping your hands light), and don't panic. Relax and enjoy yourself, and pretend you're Queen Victoria. It's a great feeling.

Once considered a thing of the past, riding sidesaddle is enjoying a new surge of popularity

Racing

Although the idea of mounting a racehorse for a spin down the track is about as far from your own sense of reality as riding a hunter sidesaddle in pursuit of a fox, don't bet on it. The open-minded opportunistic horseless rider is capable of almost anything. Take my friend Steve Price, a writer by profession, a rider by avocation and a horseless person by necessity. He was given a chance to help a famous jockey write his autobiography and off Steve went (boots and breeches in his suitcase, as always). It turns out that the book never materialized, but Steve did manage to ride an outrider's pony (a retired racer past his prime) for some exercise at Santa Anita. A slow gallop was all that the horse needed ('Sure,' says Steve, 'like a Maserati full throttle!'), and once around the track was all that Steve needed to know that this form of transportation had to be as fast as anything he'd ever known, jet age or no. I, too, have had my experiences in the backstretch, the most exciting of which was a spin around a training track aboard a three-year-old colt under the watchful eye of his trainer and an exercise rider who poised himself on a pony at the edge of the track just in case I got into trouble. The colt was an enormous, powerful animal, full of oats and eagerness to run, and I was apprehensive, to say the least, since I felt as though I was sitting on a coiled spring with only my sense of balance to keep me in place. After a few moments of walking to the track, however, I realized that this was, after all, a horse like any other, responsive to legs, hands and voice, and that my previous riding experience was perfectly applicable. The stirrups were shorter than I expected, and the reins had to be held differently (race horses do not have sensitive mouths but need a strong pair of hands supported by body weight), but the basic principles were the same. Although my facial expression for those few minutes around the track revealed (I was told later) more fear than delight, my confidence did not elude me entirely and the experience was exhilarating. I don't have the time or the inclination to become a professional exercise rider, but I can enthusiastically recommend the backstretch for those who do. (See page 199 for information about the professional side of this world.)

Everyone who has ever seen a horse race knows that the stirrups have to be as short as humanly possible and that one's position must be as far into the horse's mane as one can manage. But actually, the exercise jockeys aren't as extreme in position as the real jockeys in a race. After all, a horse being galloped in its daily routine doesn't need to go like the wind, only like a jet plane, and the jockeys don't need to weigh as little as children to make them move. The idea of the jockey's position is to create as little wind resistance as possible and to stay forward in order to free the hindquarters to do their stuff and to keep the horse's balance over its forelegs. But there are some other techniques worth knowing by the occasional rider — not for real race horses but for the occasional former racer who has somehow found his way into private or public life as a saddle horse. The tighter you hold the reins, the faster the horse is likely to go. This isn't just a matter of training, since any unschooled or poorly schooled horse given a certain amount of resistance will try to fight it. This natural inclination is what trainers exploit in working with their animals: resist with the hands and you're off to the races. Another racing technique is to keep your weight in the stirrups rather than in your upper thighs and seat. This means that the rider has precious little security and control, but that's what makes horse races so exciting. Actually, racing jockeys must have some control over their mounts in order to rate them (get them to run faster or slower) and to push them into strategic positions for the stretch run. In addition to the whip, the jockey uses his voice, the reins (to change leads or direction) and his hands, which can urge a horse forward when they are moved up on the horse's neck. Beyond that, the jockey must use his eyes to avoid running into other horses and to gauge his own position on the track (by recognizing the track poles as he rides by), and his wits, which must be as sharp as tacks. One jockey told me that reactions must be instantaneous in making decisions; if you have to think about what you're going to do, it will already be too late!

Steeplechasing, or race riding over fences, may seem similar

Riding a racehorse can be a lucrative and exciting career

to the cross-country phase of combined training, since speed is the deciding factor, but actually the two are distinct, if only because steeplechasing or point-to-point racing involves competition against other horses and three-day riders compete only with the clock. Also, with a few notable exceptions, the obstacles in a steeplechase are far less demanding than those in a cross-country course. But steeplechasing nonetheless is probably one of the most demanding and dangerous sports from the rider's point of view because the fences – some of them as high as five and a half feet or as wide as six feet – must be negotiated at racing speed. This means that each jump must be approached perfectly in stride to avoid bad take-offs, and this necessitates perfect timing and control on the part of the rider as well as a certain amount of savvy on the part of the animal. This is a sport to be avoided by all but the most experienced or foolhardy, but one can still learn a good deal by watching a steeplechase in action. Note how the riders often sit back while taking a jump, rather than forward in the classic jumping position. This is not to help the horse (who needs very little enforced impulsion since he's going at full speed) but to help the rider stay in place. This is known as the security seat and, not surprisingly, it resembles the position taken by fox-hunters in those famous old prints and paintings. (You'll also see it over drop fences in cross-country events.) It's not very pretty, and it's not particularly good for the horse, but it is much safer than landing on a horse's neck (or worse, ahead of the horse on the other side of the jump).

Although race riding is particularly demanding in these ways, the methods that jockeys use are both natural and universal, which is what makes it possible for Lester Pigott and the others to ride horses that they have never seen before.

9
Full-time Horsemanship

This chapter is devoted to those horseless riders who have allowed horse fever to get completely out of hand. They are the dedicated, the obsessed, the incurable. Prevention is no cure at this point. What you need is treatment, pure and simple, and that treatment has to take the form of a full-time commitment to horses. There are two courses open to you – becoming a professional, if you must remain horseless, or becoming a horse owner.

Professional Horsemanship

We have talked about part-time jobs as a way of getting more rides, free rides or simply learning the basics of stable management and horse care. Becoming a professional, however, involves a full-time dedication, whether this means a formal, salaried position or a freelance activity repaid in the form of commissions or occasional windfalls. Whatever your situation, you can't expect to start at the top – or even halfway up the ladder – until you have had sufficient experience from the ground up and some good basic education in the field. The British Horse Society publishes a pamphlet describing the programmes and careers available to those who wish to train for work with horses, and it is well worth reading for there are many opportunities.

Instruction

The BHS recommends that one begin by preparing for the first professional BHS examination – the BHS Assistant Instructor's Certificate – which requires a student to be at least seventeen-and-a-half years old with 4 'O' level passes at Grade

C or better (one of which must be an English language course) or an equivalent qualification. There are four sections of this examination that must be passed: equitation, stable management, minor ailments and instruction. Then one may go to an Intermediate Instructor's Certificate, the Intermediate Teaching Certificate, the Instructor's Certificate and eventually the BHS Fellowship, for which one is examined in equitation, training and ability as an instructor. One may study for these examinations at any approved riding school that offers programmes for career students, and it is also possible to apply for grants to cover both tuition and lodging. If you apply for a grant, you will be sent to one of five selection centres in the country where a special board will evaluate you as an applicant. Most schools run intensive courses for paying students, residential and non-residential, but some also offer a means for students to work at the school in return for tuition or for board and lodging. Courses may last from three to fifteen months. Working students are advised to obtain a written contract and to examine both living and working facilities before taking up employment.

Horse-related courses for those who do not necessarily wish to pursue instruction as a career are also available, but before we look at those, let's take a glance at what a riding instructor's life is like. Riding instruction runs the gamut from giving friendly advice gratis to highly paid coaching jobs. Sometimes a talented rider will turn to instruction because people are willing to pay for the chance to learn his or her techniques, but most instructors in the country are trained to teach as well as to ride. It is one thing to be able to ride well, but it is quite another to convey to a rider what is wrong and what can be done to make it right. A teacher must be observant, articulate, patient and knowledgable about both horses and people.

The rewards of teaching are varied; some instructors are satisfied only if their students win blue rosettes, while others are delighted just to know that a frightened beginner has achieved some self-confidence and the ability to master a rising trot. Very special instructors devote themselves to teaching handicapped people to ride; others specialize in extremely advanced forms of competitive riding. Some instructors are paid a salary, while others receive a commission on the basis of the number of students they teach. Most teachers, however, do their job more for love rather than for money.

Instructors may work every day from dawn to dusk teaching beginners, or they may work once a month giving special clinics at different stables to a handful of riders. Any instructor should have the ability to work with a beginner who has never been on a horse, but the job will be more interesting if beginner classes can be alternated with intermediate and advanced instruction. In a busy stable, one must be flexible enough to conduct a group lesson of several students as well as private lessons with one or two riders. Whether one devises a lesson 'plan' at the beginning of each class or simply plays the lesson by ear will depend on the riders as well as the instructors, as will the type and level of riding that is taught. In addition to knowing the capabilities and limitations of each student, the instructor must also know his or her school horses intimately in order to assign them to individual students. Reschooling sour horses, schooling green ones and dealing with difficult situations during a class will require that the instructor ride or present a 'show-not-tell' session. A few instructors I know call out commands and corrections from the centre of the school; some will give mini-lectures before or after the students ride; some yell at mistakes while others speak softly and reassuringly; many instructors concentrate on one thing at a time (legs, hands, seat) while others work on the total picture; some aim for an attractive appearance and self-confidence in their riders, while others work toward developing flexibility and courage on more demanding and varied animals.

As well as knowing students, horses and the theories and methods of instruction, an instructor must also be capable of dealing with the demands of the show ring or the competitive aspects of the sport. This means that he or she should know when a student is ready to compete and be prepared to coach the rider through the great event – selecting the appropriate classes and the horse, giving last-minute instructions and advice, and following up with praise, constructive criticism and encouragement for the next time. At your first few shows, the psychological influence of the instructor can be far more important than any specific instruction. I recall one equitation class in which I was riding a new horse and concentrating very hard on my diagonals and leads and so on; when I looked over at my instructor to see how I was doing, he simply said 'Smile!' Suddenly I relaxed and began to enjoy myself, presenting a far more confident appearance to the judge than I had been doing. In the same show, however, jumping the same unfamiliar horse over a newly set up course of fences I had never seen, my instructor was called away at the last minute by another contestant just as I entered the show ring. So I had to memorize the course fast and jump it with no real idea of what I was doing. Needless to say, my nervousness transmitted itself to the horse and we didn't do very well.

In other words, the instructor is more than simply a human riding manual. He or she must assume a certain amount of psychological responsibility for students – building up self-confidence, developing a sense of reality and a respect for hard work, and emphasizing attitude as well as ability. The relationship between teacher and student (and often the student's family as well) can be the making or breaking of the student's future as a horseman. Many talented beginners have been put off riding by an insensitive or indifferent teacher, while other less apt pupils have developed into fine horsemen just because they had the encouragement and information given them at a crucial stage in their development.

Stable Management

This is an important aspect of an instructor's education – anyone involved in teaching horsemanship must know the basics of horse care – but as a career, stable management is often an end in itself. Most small stables are run by the owner, but any sizeable operation generally employs someone to act on the owner's behalf to take care of the myriad details: ordering feed, bedding and equipment; seeing that the proper goods are delivered on time and properly stored; hiring, supervising and firing stable help; setting up and managing courses of lessons; charging customers; arranging for vans to transport incoming and outgoing horses; dealing with vets and farriers; and running special events, such as shows, lectures or films, and other programmes. If the stable is primarily interested in hacking or instruction, the manager may be responsible for finding and purchasing suitable horses and for deciding which horses are to be offered to which riders. It is the manager's responsibility to see that the horses are cared for properly, that customers are satisfied and that the money comes in and goes out in a businesslike way.

The job is not a simple one and requires a good head for organization and administration, as well as the ability to get along with people. More important, it requires a great deal of knowledge about horses and what is meant by good care. A background in stable work is essential, since a good manager must know how a stable works from the bottom up, but direct experience in riding is also important as well as a working knowledge of health care, food quality, horseshoeing and first aid. It is also useful to have good contacts beyond the stable itself with dealers, feed suppliers, instructors and other professionals in the field.

Some stable managers double as instructors or take charge of the lessons; others concentrate on breeding and must be familiar not only with the management of stallions, broodmares and foals, but also with the roles of matchmaker, midwife, nurse, trainer and salesman. Often a stable manager will be the trainer with individual animals to care for in addition to the operation of the stable itself.

The British Horse Society Instructor's Certificate is given not only in teaching but also in stable management, an examination for which may be taken at twenty-two years of age following the acquisition of the Assistant Instructor's and Intermediate Instructor's Certificates. A number of schools offer excellent courses in stable management. The National

Certificate in Agriculture for Women is run at Brackenhurst in Nottinghamshire and includes in the year's syllabus three hours a week in horse management and riding. Warwickshire College of Agriculture at Moreton Morrell offers a horse management course as well as a horse business management course. Those interested in a college certificate in stud and stable management may apply for a one-year course to the Department of Agriculture, West Oxfordshire Technical College, Witney, Oxfordshire.

Stable employees not interested in the administrative responsibilities that go with a manager's job can, of course, work as assistant managers or grooms – or in a special capacity as show manager, scout for new horses and so on. In many stables the job of groom is a career in itself, not a stepping stone to something else, and good grooms are probably the most valuable members of the staff in a well-run stable. In very large stables, there are often head grooms, who supervise the work of those who attend to a certain number of animals – from one to ten apiece – but it is the individual groom on whom the veterinary surgeon relies for essential information about a horse's symptoms and unusual changes in behaviour, on whom the farrier relies for assistance, on whom riders count for tips about temperament and habits, and on whom the trainers and owners depend for general equine well-being.

For it is the groom who knows the horse inside and out. He or she is constantly alert to the animal's condition and should be the first to note any situation that may require an adjustment in feed or a call to the vet or farrier. The groom must be skilled also in the fine art of bandaging legs, applying medications, removing or readjusting horse shoes – in short, doing a great deal more than simply grooming. The Association of British Riding Schools has an examination called the Groom's Diploma; you can obtain information by writing to the Association at Chesham House, 56 Green End Road, Sawtry, Huntingdon, Cambridgeshire. Young people who are especially interested in learning to work around a racing stable may attend a series of courses at Goodwood, for which details are available from the Jockey Club (Registry Office, 42 Portman Square, London W1).

Two further important aspects of stable management require special training: veterinary work and horseshoeing. Licensed veterinary surgeons must study in medical school and the field is a very competitive one; not all vets go into equine work but many limit their practices to dogs and cats, to exotic and wild animals, to cattle and other farm animals. Equine practitioners are specialists within the field, and a summer holiday spent working as an assistant to a horse doctor can be a marvellous experience for anyone seriously interested in pursuing this extremely demanding field as a career. A somewhat less demanding career in this field is that of animal nursing auxiliary, for which courses are given. For information about veterinary work, write to the Royal College of Veterinary Surgeons, 32 Belgrave Square, London SW1.

Blacksmiths who work with horses prefer to be called farriers (to distinguish themselves from those who make iron grillework and gates and such). They, too, must learn their trade by specialized study, though this needn't be in a formal school but can be as an apprentice to an expert. There are several good books on the subject and it is possible to learn a lot by watching a farrier at work; but it will take practice before you can become expert yourself. In addition to learning about the craft of working with metal and using a forge, you will have to learn an enormous amount about horse conformation and movement, since shoeing these days involves a great deal more than making shoes fit. Corrective shoeing has helped turn many poor performers into stars and many useful animals into valuable ones. For information about their four-year apprenticeship scheme, write to the Worshipful Company of Farriers, 3 Hamilton Road, Cockfosters, Barnet, Hertfordshire.

Professional Riding

Although most horseless riders pay for the privilege, riders who are talented or opportunistic enough can have their cake and eat it, too – spending their careers in the saddle and getting paid for it besides. Riders who wish to maintain their amateur status for the sake of showing in amateur classes or competing in the Olympic Games cannot accept money either as a salary or in the form of prizes, and amateurs over the age of eighteen must be extremely careful about obeying the rules of amateurism. But riders without special ambitions can earn money in any number of different ways.

Race track trainers employ exercise riders to get their horses into condition and keep them that way. Both men and women can get these jobs, so long as their weight is within reason (one hundred to one hundred and twenty-five pounds, depending on the horse and the trainer), and they are capable of following instructions as well as handling lively, strong, young animals. Having a good sense of timing or being experienced in using timeclocks is an important part of the job, too, as is the ability to adapt one's style to many different kinds and temperaments of horses. Exercise for flat racers may vary from easy gallops to breezes (which are faster) to real work-outs that are timed by the clockers and published in the racing sheets read by punters. Exercise for steeplechasers can be anything from long steady gallops across country (up and down hills, along beaches and so on) to concentrated work over fences. Many exercise riders work on salary, although freelancers will work for a certain sum per horse exercised (usually a pound or two, although it can be twice that for problem horses). The salaried rider may not make as much money but often prefers the steady employment and the chance to ride the same horses every day. Some riders are young and looking forward to the time when they can become licensed jockeys, though many riders have no such ambitions or have already been through the jockey stage, having gained too much weight or lost too many races.

Another race track job is that of the pony-rider or outrider, who fulfills an important service to both trainers and jockeys before and after races and during training sessions. These riders are mounted on relatively undistinguished animals, but their presence on the backstretch is invaluable. Their mounts are not usually ponies in the technical sense (under fourteen-

and-a-half hands in height) but are full-grown horses that are used to 'pony' or lead young race horses out to the post before races or around training tracks during the morning gallops. Horses are, of course, herd animals by nature, and it is not surprising that nervous adolescent equines are reassured when escorted by older, wiser horses with steady temperaments. Perhaps more important, however, is the fact that these ponies are capable of quick bursts of speed necessary to catch runaways or eager beavers who continue to run their races long past the finish line. Horses bred to run often don't know enough to stop – nor can they be controlled when straps break or riders lack the strength or weight to pull them in. The outrider stationed along the edge of the track can therefore play a crucial role in stopping a valuable animal before it runs itself into the ground. A trainer friend of mine owns an old pony, one that many other trainers would have given up on years earlier and sold off to a hacking stable or relegated to some other obscure occupation. Old Billygoat, however, has saved the life of more than one talented racer and will be assured of a comfortable life around the race track as long as he lives, which may well be for another ten years, since, like many ponies, he is blessed with more determination than anything else.

Pony-rider or outrider jobs are usually paid on a freelance basis, in that trainers will pay a fee to them for their services, but some of these positions are salaried, either by trainers or by the race tracks. Although the idea of being mounted on an old grade gelding isn't so glamorous when everyone around you is riding an elegant young speedster, the responsibility involved is a very important one and many lives, both horse and human, have been saved by the quick action taken on the part of the outrider.

Off the race track, riders may be employed by trainers who need help in schooling a stableful of horses, by stable managers who are paid by owners to keep their horses fit as well as fed, and by dealers who want someone to show off a saleable beast to best advantage. Advanced students may work for their instructors; grooms can double as exercise riders; trusted customers may work for their rides by helping out around the hack stable. In short, if you have the talent, the time and the energy, you can probably find yourself gainful employment by riding for more than simple pleasure. If an owner is pleased with a rider's performance on the horse (or, more likely, the horse's performance under the rider), the next step may mean going into horse shows or other forms of competition for which the rider is paid. 'Catch-riding', as I have mentioned earlier, is an excellent way for a rider to build up a reputation and to get backing or support for a career in the show ring. The better the reputation, the better the horses one is likely to be offered, and this requires, of course, a great deal of adaptability as well as pure talent. The American Rodney Jenkins, who has earned more money as a professional rider than anyone else on the hunter-jumper circuit, often finds himself mounting a horse for the first time moments before entering the show ring, and he frequently rides several horses in each class. I asked him how he could possibly keep the different, unfamiliar animals straight in his mind, to say nothing of straight on the course. He explained that since childhood he was always given the 'leftover' horses in his father's stable to ride and that he has ridden so many horses in his career that he has developed a sixth sense about them. He can tell in a few hundred feet of trotting what a horse's potential may be and he knows what he will be like over fences by taking only a couple of schooling jumps. Jenkins relies almost entirely on balance (rather than strong hands, different kinds of bits and so on) and says that keeping his balance on a horse is the best way to get the most out of him.

Any public stable that hires horses to beginners for trail rides must employ one or more guides to see that everyone makes it back in one piece, and the trail guide's responsibility is a serious one. The guide must be able to handle his or her own horse properly because there are many other things that must be watched and also because the novice riders will be watching the guide in order to learn something. The guide must see that each rider in the group is handling the horse correctly (which usually involves an instant, on-the-spot lesson), that all riders stay in suitable formation, that traffic laws are obeyed and public roads safely crossed and that emergencies are dealt with promptly and efficiently. In other words, the guide must be teacher, disciplinarian, object lesson, traffic policeman and nurse, as well as horseman. Many stables I've visited have had indifferent guides who are inexperienced with both people and horses, and nothing is more frustrating than taking orders from someone who doesn't know the difference between a hip and a hock. But I've always been glad to have a guide along, if only because it shows that the stable cares to some extent about the safety of their customers, and of course, it's always possible to pick up information from the guide about trails and individual horses so that the next ride out alone will not result in getting lost or run away with.

Anyone who knows how to ride could probably get a job as a guide, but he or she must be prepared to do more than just ride, and being able to tell a prospective employer that you have a solid grounding in first aid, instruction and/or stable management will give you a definite advantage over other prospective candidates for employment.

Someone with experience as a trail guide who also has a passion for dogs (or hounds) and enjoys the tradition of fox-hunting, can work as a member of the hunt staff, as a whipper-in or a huntsman, which in many areas are professional occupations. You must, of course, know horses, the territory, and the rules and traditions of the sport, but you must also get involved in breeding and training fox hounds, which, for some, is a refreshing supplement to full-time horsemanship.

Mounted policemen are policemen first and horsemen second, but anyone who wants to combine careers can have the best of both worlds in this line of work.

Training

The ancient art of training horses goes hand in hand with instructing riders, but the emphasis here is on the horse, and the opportunities for a fine trainer are far greater than those for one who concentrates on riding alone. It is essential to be a horseman through and through – understanding all aspects of horse selection, horse care and horse psychology – as well as being capable of administering a staff, dealing with owners, and knowing every detail of the particular business, whether it be racing, showing or preparing horses for pleasure riding. In competition, a trainer must know the opposition as well as his own animals and must be able to carry out his own theories in practice effectively. He should know what he wants before he starts and be willing to do whatever is necessary to reach that goal, whether it means schooling one horse (or a dozen) every day for an hour himself or relying on capable assistants to follow instructions.

Obviously, the background for an aspiring trainer should be in as many different aspects of the horse business as possible – from stable management to horse dealing – but a definite prerequisite is that of working with animals and being able to bring out the best in them. This means that the trainer must know what a horse is capable of doing and the most effective ways of teaching it to do those things. Understanding a horse's physical and psychological limitations is a very complicated business, and while it comes naturally to some people who are born with what can only be described as horse sense, it can be developed through years of experience. Some trainers are riders; others never get on the back of a horse; some have an 'eye' for a potentially good animal; others make do with what they get and still others get into breeding in order to create what they want.

A trainer should, of course, understand what it is that the owner of a horse wants, but be knowledgeable and strong-minded and persuasive enough to convince the owner that the trainer knows best. The best owners are those who will rely on the judgement of their trainers, and there are many unhappy stories about misunderstandings or struggles for authority that have resulted in lost jobs or poor performances by the animals caught in the middle. The trainer must accept the responsibility when the horse in his charge does poorly, but he is the one who can take most of the credit when the horse does well. Although the monetary rewards can be great for a few, money is not usually the ultimate goal for a trainer, whose long hours and constant worries couldn't be reckoned in pounds, regardless of the talent of the accountant.

Horse Dealing

Buying and selling horses is a profession that has been around as long as there have been horses to buy and sell, and of all the horse-related occupations, it is probably the most controversial. Horse traders have been subject to more bad jokes and wonderful stories than any other kind of horsemen. Through the ages, horse traders have been despised and hanged, trusted and respected, accused of stealing or misrepresenting their animals, and praised for their perceptions. Yet horse owners and riders couldn't possibly exist without them. You can, of course, come across an advertisement describing a horse for sale and simply buy it without using a dealer, but people in the market for special kinds of horses can't rely on local newspapers or gossip as sources for what they need. It is the job of the dealer to find animals and to get them into the hands of the people who will pay for them, and for performing this service the dealer receives a commission of the selling price from the seller or the buyer; he may also get his money by buying horses and reselling them at higher prices, or he may simply get a slice of another dealer's commission by having referred a buyer or a seller. Anyone involved in the purchase of a horse can be a dealer. Sometimes stable managers and trainers are dealers themselves and sometimes a dealer may not be a horseman at all. All one needs is a sense of what a horse is worth, a source for animals, and a list of potential clients. Many dealers go further, having an animal schooled for a particular purpose or a particular buyer, buying a few yearlings each year from breeders or at auctions and putting a sizeable investment into getting them ready for sale a year or more later.

Although stories are legion about gypsy horse traders who paint white horses black and who feed tranquilizers to highly strung rogues, most dealers must be honest if they are to stay in business. There are laws governing the sale of horses and anyone who routinely disobeys those laws – selling unsuitable animals under false claims – will be in trouble legally as well as professionally.

In addition to knowing about horses, dealers must know a great deal about people in order to analyse what a potential owner really wants (often not what the buyer says) and how to present the animal in a convincing way. Many dealers will go to a lot of trouble grooming a horse, getting a good rider to show it off, and sometimes even having the animal reschooled. Newcomers to the profession often find themselves severely out of pocket because they have misread the requirements of a buyer; I have been known dealers taken in by people who make a hobby of getting free rides by 'trying out' one horse after another with no intention of making a purchase. Other dealers will spend months looking for the perfect horse when the buyer really needs to be convinced that a less-than-perfect animal would be quite satisfactory. Indecisive and unknowledgeable buyers, the bane of a dealer's existence, are unfortunately far more common than unscrupulous dealers.

A dealer must, naturally, be completely aware of what certain types of horses are worth in order to set prices that are in line with the market. Since the name of the game is making money, one can't be too sentimental about animals or make the mistake of falling in love with a particular horse unless he is prepared to keep it. He must also be prepared to accept 'returns' – horses that haven't worked out for one reason or another. He must be ready to make a decision to have an unsaleable horse put to death or sold for meat, or to watch another dealer make a bundle reselling a horse on which he may have only made a few pounds. It's not an easy business, but the rewards are perhaps more easily banked than they are in other professions.

Owning a Horse

Up to this point, every word in the book you've been reading has been directed to the rider who doesn't own his own horse, and you should be by now convinced that 'horselessness' has as many advantages as challenges to offer. Nevertheless, I suspect that deep down inside each reader still remains that residual, repressed desire to own one of the infernal creatures in spite of all the problems involved. (I admit that I've always had a saddle and bridle on hand just in case.) When I was a child, I used to enter contests that offered horses as prizes, though all I ever won was a pretty silver crayon in a colouring competition. I used to write delightful, if thankfully forgotten, lyrics to celebrate things like the birth of the Black Stallion's daughter for whom I did not, however, select the winning name. I suppose I always hoped that if a free horse should happen to turn up in the front garden with reporters and photographers in tow, my parents would be somehow embarrassed into keeping the animal just to keep the family reputation intact.

Although we all by now know that the purchase price of a horse is the least of the investment (unless you are prepared to spend several thousand pounds for a fine show horse or for a fetlock of Red Rum's), and that any horse, regardless of price, will cost far more to keep over the long run than on the day of purchase, it has always been my philosophy that it is folly not to enter some contest – any contest – that will make one a horse owner, even if only briefly.

However, there are other inexpensive ways to come by a perfectly respectable animal, even if it isn't a purebred Arab or a daughter of the Black Stallion. Mounted police departments in many cities retire their animals to farms where they will be given a good home, and school horses that can no longer work the necessary four or five hours a day can often be picked up for very little indeed. It may take a good deal of reschooling, resting and reassuring to turn these well-used beasts into good pleasure horses, but it's been done. The parents of children who have gone off to school or gone off horses can be approached with a 'let me take that burden off your hands' attitude, and professionals with show horses past their prime may be more willing to let their animals go to a conscientious individual than to a public stable or out to pasture. These horses may be spoiled in some way – by injury, overuse, neglect or overindulgence – but the determined and experienced amateur can often remake them into very satisfactory mounts, give time and patience.

If you find yourself with a gift horse on your hands, do look in its mouth (and everywhere else you and the vet can think of) to make sure you are not also getting a future filled with worries and vet bills (or doctor bills for yourself). But if the horse is potentially a good one and you are willing to do what it takes (or not do anything but let it get a good rest until it's back in shape), there are a number of ways to keep your maintenance expenses to a minimum and still guarantee the horse good care.

Leasing

How about hiring a horse for a year rather than just an hour? Many owners who do not have the opportunity to ride are willing to let a trusted individual have complete use of the horse without selling it. The hirer in this case will agree to pay all maintenance expenses – boarding, feed, vet bills, horseshoes, etc. – and the horse is effectively theirs without any initial investment in its ownership. This arrangement may sound ideal, but it can be fraught with danger if the agreement is not made in writing to cover contingencies such as accident or loss of the horse. The hirer must be sure that he or she will not be held liable if the animal should suddenly take ill and die or be severely injured or killed in an accident. The hirer should also try to get the owner to agree to a certain amount of notice should the horse be sold. It would be a very disheartening situation to have 'your' horse win a blue rosette and be sold from under you to someone who noticed him at the show. All your schooling and work might have doubled the value of the horse and you'd have nothing to show for it, not even the horse.

Co-leasing, or sharing the expenses with a partner, is even more complicated, for although the cost to you is halved, the amount of time you can use the horse is halved as well. In addition to an agreement with the owner, you should have one with your partner so that there won't be arguments about which days you had access to the animal and who caused what saddle sores. Many friendships have been broken because these details weren't worked out ahead of time. I was once offered half a horse for a third of the cost, but it turned out that the horse needed more than the usual amount of veterinary care and my veterinarian husband made me a pretty attractive partner. My husband would have had to spend more time with the animal than I would have, so I said no.

Co-owning

Like hiring, co-owning a horse with someone else can be an attractive economic arrangement but a complicated one if nothing is put in writing. Again, it should be made clear at the outset exactly what is to be expected by way of responsibility, expense and accessibility. In addition, it should be understood that both riders won't try to expect too much from the horse; it would be silly and impractical for one rider to school an animal in dressage while the other rider spends alternate days trying to 'uncollect' him. Specific schedules for the care of the horse should be worked out in detail so that nothing gets overlooked, and someone should be responsible for regular appointments with the vet and the farrier, and for ordering feed and bedding. Another part of the agreement should cover the contingency of accident or illness, and last but not least, the mechanics of withdrawing from the arrangement in case one owner moves away or loses interest should also be considered. In such cases the question of whether the horse is sold and the profit split, or whether one owner will buy out the other seems to be a simple decision until the situation actually arises without prior consideration having been given to the matter.

Some co-ownership arrangements involve a 'silent partner', who foots the bills, and a rider, who enters the horse in competitions to further the animal's career and boost its value. Here, too, agreements must be in writing – even down to tiny details such as who keeps the rosettes, trophies and prize money, who decides about which shows to enter, and who gets what share of the profits if the horse is sold.

Owning

In some 'silent partner' arrangements, the one who pays the bills actually owns the horse while the rider simply gets a share of the winnings and profits rather than a salary or even expenses. In other cases, the rider is simply a hired employee who earns a salary and/or expenses without making any investment except that of skill and time. But what about owning a horse and wanting to ride it while saving some money by letting other people ride? Many people keep their horses at livery stables and allow the managers or instructors use of the animals in return for discounts on livery fees. The decision to do this is not to be made without serious consideration. What if the animal is soured by constant jabs in the mouth delivered by beginners? What if the horse is injured or, worse, what if a rider is injured and sues the owner of the horse, now you, for damages? This kind of arrangement may work beautifully if you trust the stable operator or instructor and are insured to cover any contingencies, but the owner has to be aware of these possibilities before entering into any such agreement.

I have always disapproved of absentee owners who selfishly keep animals to themselves but not *for* themselves. I have often ridden private horses in lessons with their trainers and have been delighted by the experience; I've also been told that such an experience can be good for a horse who would otherwise get only an occasional lungeing or a brief schooling session, since that's all the trainer has time to give. But I can understand the owner's point of view as well. Because of the risks involved, it is a good idea to be able to have some control over the use of your animal – whether it is through a trusted trainer or by direct means.

What this boils down to, of course, is that if you are going to own a horse, you should take the time and trouble to keep it well and fit. But if you want a trophy room full of rosettes and silver cups and you can't ride well enough yourself, you will have to let someone else do the riding for you. And if you want to keep the horse in peak condition, and can't afford the daily hour or more to exercise it yourself, you will have to hire, or persuade, someone else to spend the time for you. In other words, if you own a riderless horse, get a horseless rider for it. Like my friend with the boarding stable in California, remember your horseless days and do unto others as others once did unto you.

Epilogue

Shortly after I finished the manuscript for this book, I had the great good fortune to be offered a gift horse. I thought to myself that accepting this animal would not be a denial of my enthusiasm for horselessness but a legitimate experience and perhaps even the subject for an upbeat, inspiring ending to my book. The horse was a four-year-old chestnut thoroughbred gelding, as unschooled as he was gorgeous, and completely unsuited to his owner, who felt that I could provide him with a good home and an education at the same time. I read all the training manuals and made out that shopping list I had dreamed of making for years (the kind that begins 'one halter, one currycomb . . .'). I located an empty stall in a nearby stable, hired a van to truck the horse there, and then made the mistake of trying him out before putting him in the van. The inside of his mouth looked fine to me (I wasn't stupid enough to obey *that* old gift-horse maxim) but his outward behaviour was erratic enough to convince me that there might be a reason he was completely untrained at the age of four. He was – to put it mildly – disrespectful of humans, in need of a strong professional trainer rather than an enthusiastic amateur. He was, in other words, as unsuitable for me as he was for his owner. So, heavy in heart, I ripped up my list and rejoined the ranks of the horseless, happy only in the fact that I had come to my senses before he came into my possession.

Needless to say, my happy ending for the book was suddenly as empty as that stall, until I realized the following weekend that everything wasn't as bleak as it seemed. On Saturday morning I helped someone to reschool a talented but sour jumper; Sunday morning found me riding a three-year-old colt at the race track under the supervision of a trainer friend; and on Sunday afternoon I spent two hours working with a former race horse that had enlisted in the local mounted police unit. By Sunday evening, it dawned on me that the horseless life had its moments, that none of this would have been possible if I had made the commitment to a horse of my own. Perhaps my good luck that weekend was a kind of coincidental compensation for my bad luck with the gift horse, but I prefer to believe that my commitment to horselessness was what had opened up those opportunities in the first place. In fact, judging from my schedule for the next month, I can see that my life is going to be no less interesting: a 'lunch' date exercising a holidaying friend's thoroughbred at the local city stable; a day in the country fox-hunting with one of the oldest packs in the country. And that, I have a distinct feeling, is only a taste of what lies ahead.

Acknowledgements

If I were to thank in print all of the instructors – human and equine –
who have helped me through years of horselessness, the list would be
longer than any reader could bear, but the following individuals
deserve special mention for assistance beyond the call of
friendship:

Lou Accurso
Allegro
Bedford
Bigfoot and Billygoat
Bill Brayton
Dennis Byrnes
Harry Case
Michael Cody
Helene Conway
Jim Conway
Copperhead
Martina D'Alton
Anthony D'Ambrosio, Jr.
Bill Decker
Norman dello Joio
Eugene Edwinn
Carlos Estol
Susan Goode
Susan Heath
Hoffman
Chris Howells
Geoffrey Hughes
Rodney Jenkins
Charlie and Sandra Kauffman
King

Alexander and Marilyn
   Mackay-Smith
Wingate Mackay-Smith
Carlos Marban
Rebecca Martin
Martini
Catherine McWilliams
Kay Meredith
Joanne Michaels
Darryl Montoya
Jill Murphy
Bertalan de Nemethy
Amy Pershing
Evelyn Pervier
Phoebe Phillips
Elric Pinckney
Gail and Werner Rentsch
Lt. Richard Risoli
Malley San Marcos
Gretchen Singleton
David Spector
Bill Steinkraus
Jerry and Rita Trapani
Amanda Vaill

In addition to these horseless riders, horses and horsemen, I would
like to give very special thanks to Steve Price, who got me back on a
horse after a lapse of ten years and gave me the idea for this book

216 ACKNOWLEDGEMENTS

(without realizing it would turn into an autobiography), and to my husband, Emil Dolensek, who has still not been able to find in his veterinary bag a cure for the disease known as horse fever.

I should also like to give a special acknowledgement to the British Horse Society for its help in the preparation of the British edition of this book. Although the Society does not specifically direct its attention to the needs of 'horseless' riders, its encouragement of better riding instruction, the humane care of horses and the improvement of equestrian activities throughout Great Britain is invaluable for all horsemen. I am particularly grateful as well to Lionel Phillips for his assistance in making the book more useful for British readers.

Index